CITYSPOTS
MILAN

Barbara Radcliffe Rogers
& Stillman Rogers

Written and photographed by Barbara Radcliffe Rogers & Stillman Rogers
Front cover photography courtesy of Giovanni Simeone/4cornersimages.com
Series design based on an original concept by Studio 183 Limited

Produced by Cambridge Publishing Management Limited
Project Editor: Catherine Burch
Layout: Paul Queripel
Maps: PC Graphics
Transport map: © Communicarta Ltd

Published by Thomas Cook Publishing
A division of Thomas Cook Tour Operations Limited
Company Registration No. 1450464 England
PO Box 227, Unit 18, Coningsby Road
Peterborough PE3 8SB, United Kingdom
email: books@thomascook.com
www.thomascookpublishing.com
+44 (0)1733 416477
ISBN-13: 978-1-84157-637-4
ISBN-10: 1-84157-637-9

First edition © 2006 Thomas Cook Publishing
Text © 2006 Thomas Cook Publishing
Maps © 2006 Thomas Cook Publishing
Series Editor/Project Editor: Kelly Anne Pipes
Production/DTP: Steven Collins

Printed and bound in Spain by GraphyCems

All rights reserved. No part of this publication may be reproduced, stored in a retrieval system or transmitted, in any form or by any means, electronic, mechanical, recording or otherwise, in any part of the world, without prior permission of the publisher. Requests for permission should be made to the publisher at the above address.

Although every care has been taken in compiling this publication, and the contents are believed to be correct at the time of printing, Thomas Cook Tour Operations Limited cannot accept any responsibility for errors or omission, however caused, or for changes in details given in the guidebook, or for the consequences of any reliance on the information provided. Descriptions and assessments are based on the author's views and experiences when writing and do not necessarily represent those of Thomas Cook Tour Operations Limited.

CONTENTS

INTRODUCING MILAN
Introduction 6
When to go...................................8
Fashion..12
History..14
Lifestyle..16
Culture..18

MAKING THE MOST OF MILAN
Shopping......................................22
Eating & drinking......................24
Entertainment & nightlife......28
Sport & relaxation....................30
Accommodation.......................34
The best of Milan.....................40
Something for nothing...........44
When it rains.............................46
On arrival....................................48

THE CITY OF MILAN
Piazza del Duomo & East........58
Castello Sforzesco &
 Northwest Milan...................74
Southwest Milan.......................88

OUT OF TOWN TRIPS
Lake Como..................................102
Lake Maggiore..........................120

PRACTICAL INFORMATION
Directory......................................138
Useful phrases..........................152
Emergencies...............................154

INDEX 158

MAP LIST
Milan city.....................................50
Milan transport.........................54
Piazza del Duomo & East........59
Castello Sforzesco &
 Northwest Milan...................75
Southwest Milan.......................89
Lake Como..................................103
Lake Maggiore..........................121

CITYSPOTS

SYMBOLS & ABBREVIATIONS
The following symbols are used throughout this book:

⊙ address   ⊙ telephone   ⊙ fax   ⊙ email   ⊙ website address
⊙ opening times   ⊙ public transport connections   ⊙ important

The following symbols are used on the maps:
- *i* information office
- ✈ airport
- ✚ hospital
- ⊙ police station
- 🚍 bus station
- 🚆 railway station
- Ⓜ metro
- ✝ cathedral
- ❶ numbers denote featured cafés & restaurants
- ○ city
- ○ large town
- ○ small town
- ═ motorway
- — main road
- — minor road
- — railway

Hotels and restaurants are graded by approximate price as follows:
£ budget   ££ mid-range   £££ expensive

▶ *The impressive entrance to Galleria Vittorio Emanuele II*

INTRODUCING Milan

INTRODUCING MILAN

Introduction

Milan is known for being a style-savvy, hip city, perhaps best known for its cutting-edge sense of fashion and attractive, well-dressed inhabitants. But it hides its inner self well, and when you start to explore you will discover numerous other wonders, such as a surprising mix of architecture that puts art nouveau next to Gio Ponti and Renaissance splendour beside post-war international style. Maybe you will stop by a bar in the late afternoon and discover the spread of delicious snacks laid on for the taking. Take a detour past the designer shops of the Quadrilatero, or the chic boutiques of Brera, notice the tranquil green courtyards hidden behind the severest of buildings, or listen to a street performer in the mellow little Piazza Mercanti. You will soon discover that Milan has a sweet soul of its own.

You do have to know where to look; no one would be likely to stumble onto the Navigli, where the young and hip Milanese spend their evenings at canal-side cafés and clubs. Surprises are tucked into churches (one is lined in human bones, another is only half the size it appears), museums (a powerful unfinished work by Michelangelo), cemeteries, even sprawling Parco Sempione, where a dizzying tower with a hip café offers views as sweeping as those from the Duomo's rooftop.

Milan deserves a second look – and a third and a fourth. Like the oyster, it may take a while to get inside the sometimes tough and unattractive shell, but the pearl inside is worth the effort.

● *Shopping heaven inside the Galleria*

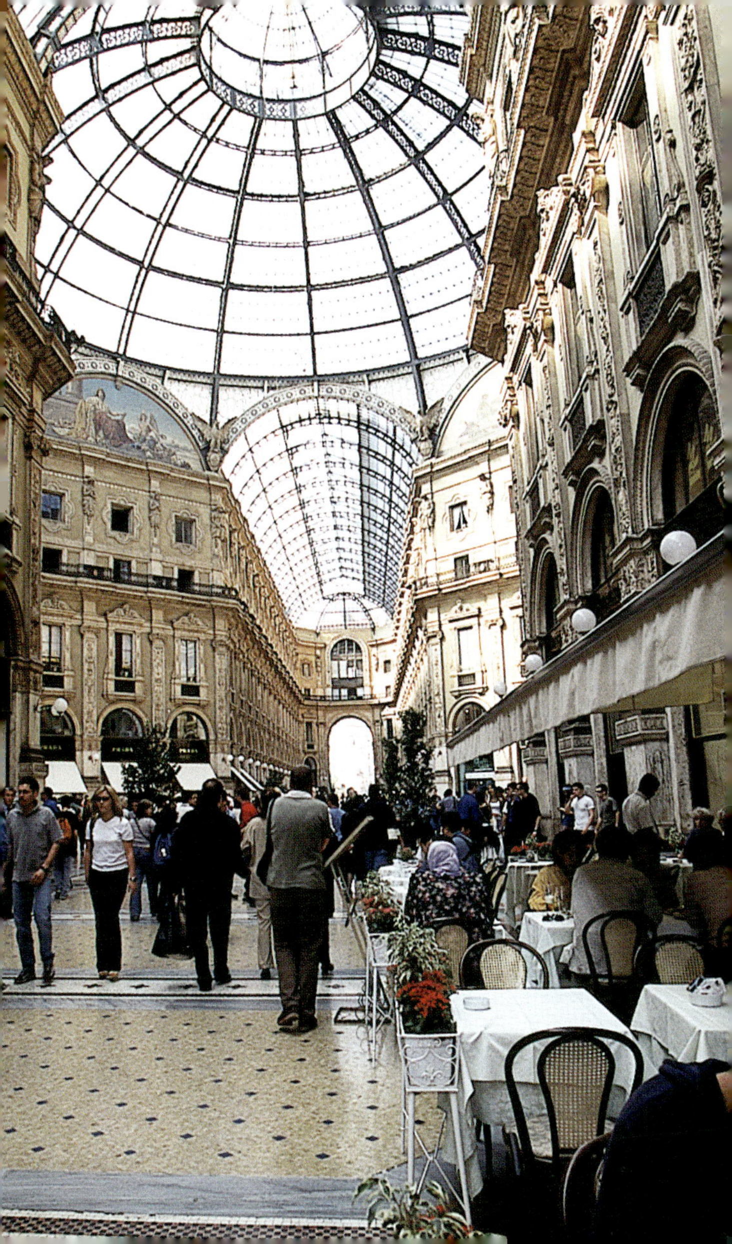

INTRODUCING MILAN

When to go

For a better chance of sampling 'sunny Italy' in Milan, go there between April and October. Take an umbrella, but expect balmy days and pleasant evenings. Real heat sets in by mid-July and by August becomes so oppressive that locals flee for the Mediterranean shore or the nearby lakes. Avoid August because all but the strictly tourist eateries (and much else in the city) are closed for the whole month. Although the weather is cooler around the lakes, hotels are packed with Milanese who've fled the sizzling streets.

Between November and March, Milan is swept by a damp icy wind blowing down from the Alps, so even the frequent sunny days are uncomfortable. When the wind lets up, a clammy fog settles over the city, sometimes for several weeks at a time. But this is the season for Milan's arts, music, performance and cultural season, so don't discount it just because of the *bruta* weather.

ANNUAL EVENTS
January
Corteo dei Re Magi (Wise Men Processional) 6 January marks the Feast of the Epiphany for the Catholic Church, and the procession begins at the Duomo at 10.00.
Milano Moda Uomo This kicks off the Italian fashion year with the autumn/winter men's collection. ⓦ www.cameramoda.com

February
Carnevale Ambrosiano A pre-Lenten bash with parades, floats and costumed folk wandering the streets around Piazza Duomo.
Milano Moda Donna Women's Fashion Week showcases Italian designers' autumn/winter styles. ⓦ www.cameramoda.com

WHEN TO GO

March
Milano-San Remo Bicycle Race The third Saturday of the month, racers pedal around the streets of the central city.
Oggi Aperto opens privately owned historic buildings for public viewing on the third weekend.
Milano International Independent Film Festival A week-long festival honouring the work of independent film-makers from around the world, at cinema venues around the city. ⓦ www.miff.it

April
Festa Di Fiori Month-long celebration of flowers and trees.
ⓐ Alzaia Naviglio Grande, Via Moscova
Stramilano Many streets close for the running of this half-marathon (15 km/9 miles). Starting places vary but are usually the Duomo or the Castello Sforzesco. ⓣ 02 8474 2380 ⓦ www.stramilano.it
Notturni in Villa A series of outdoor concerts is held at the Villa Simonetta (ⓐ Via Stilicone 36) and the Villa Litta (ⓐ Viale Affori 21), mid-April through August. Associazione Amici della Musica. ⓐ Via Boffalora ⓣ 02 8912 2383 ⓦ www.amicidellamusicamilano.it

May
Short Formats Festival A dance competition in the Palazzo dell'Arte, is part of Triennale di Milano. ⓐ Viale Alemagna 6 ⓣ 02 724 341 ⓦ www.triennale.it
Milano Cortili Aperti (Milan Open Courtyards) On a Sunday in mid-May private residence courtyards are open for public viewing, 10.00–19.00. Associazione Dimore Storiche. ⓐ Via S. Paolo 10 ⓣ 02 7631 8634 ⓦ www.italiamultimedia.com/cortiliaperti

INTRODUCING MILAN

June
Milano Moda Uomo The unveiling of spring/summer fashions for men. www.cameramoda.com
Giro d'Italia Late May or early June the grand Italian bicycle race ends in Milan. www.giroditalia.it
Festa del Naviglio A feast of concerts, processions, art, crafts, sports, food and an antique market along the Naviglio canals.
Sagra di San Christoforo (Festival of Saint Christopher) In mid-June, celebrations along the Naviglio canals, featuring decorated barges.
Milano d'Estate Sponsored public concerts in Parco Sempione, June–August.

August
Note: most restaurants and nightspots close for the entire month.

September
Le Vie del Cinema (Ways of the Cinema) Cinemas show films from the Venice Film Festival. 02 673 9781
www.lombardiaspettacolo.com
Milano Film Festival Open to young and experimental film-makers from around the world, who show short and feature films.
02 713 613 www.milanofilmfestival.it
Gran Premio di Monza The Grand Prix of Italy is held in Monza in the park setting of the Autodromo Nazionale. www.monzanet.it
Milano Moda Donna previews the cutting edge of spring/summer women's styles. www.cameramoda.com

October
Festival Milano This features contemporary music, dance, theatre, new media. 02 20 40 34 78 www.milanomusica.org

WHEN TO GO

Milano City Marathon (month may vary by year) ❶ 02 6282 8755
🌐 www.milanocitymarathon.it

November
Expo dei Sapori A grand exposition of Italian wines and foods.
📍 Fiera Milano, Padiglioni 14–16 ❶ 02 4997 7379
🌐 www.expodeisapori.it

December
La Scala Opera 7 Dec, the winter opera season opens. ❶ 02 861 827
🌐 www.teatroallascala.org
Festa di San Ambrogio Feast day, with religious celebrations and traditional fairs.
Annual Christmas Market The Piazza della Basilica di San Ambrogio hosts an extravaganza of Italian food and craft, with street performers, 09.00–21.00 daily.

> **PUBLIC HOLIDAYS**
> **New Year's Day** 1 January
> **Epiphany** 6 January
> **Easter Monday** March/April
> **Liberation Day** 25 April
> **Labour Day** 1 May
> **Republic Day** 2 June
> **Feast of the Assumption (*Ferragosto*)** 15 August
> **All Saints' Day (*Tutti i Santi*)** 1 November
> **Feast of Saint Ambrose** (patron saint of Milan) and the
> **Immaculate Conception (*Immacolata Concezione*)**
>   7–8 December
> **Christmas Day** 25 December

INTRODUCING MILAN

Fashion

Twice a year, in late February and again in late September, everybody who's anybody in Fashion (with a capital F) descends on Milan for Milano Moda Donna, Women's Fashion Week. In June and mid-January, men have their turn with Milano Moda Uomo.

Dozens of Milan designers – the cream of the fashion houses – send the top fashion models out to strut their stuff down the catwalks. It's the high point in the city's busy calendar of international design shows – furniture, food and technology are

● *Fashion is a way of life in Milan*

FASHION

just a few of the other major trade shows held here – and it sends shock waves through the clothing industry that are felt from Tokyo to New York, even (though grudgingly) in Paris.

The major houses have their own show venues, some in stunningly revamped warehouses in the old industrial sections, while the rest await their moment in the sun at the big Fiera di Milano. Known simply as Fiera, Milan's trade fair centre covers an enormous stretch of real estate west of Parco Sempione.

The catch for casual travellers without connections to the fashion industry is that you can't get into the shows without invitations. This means real credentials, not just a note on the letterhead of your hometown dress shop. The other downside is that hotel rooms are booked for months ahead of these weeks.

So why come then? You can watch it on TV and read about it in the fashion pages almost anywhere in the world, but you can't feel the buzz that changes the whole atmosphere of Milan. Hard as it is to believe, people dress even better than usual, and the clubs and bars are filled with people associated with the shows, and with others trying to get a look at them and what they are wearing. The excitement spills over to fill Milan's streets, shops and restaurants with a new electricity.

Less buzz may accompany the twice yearly men's fashion weeks, but those, too, change the city, as drop-dead gorgeous models hit town and Milanese men take extra time to choose their shirts and knot their neckties.

Just so you know where to watch, the Four Seasons Hotel is the pet digs for the international fashionistas. Any time of year, if you're anybody worth the sales clerks' attention, you simply have your designer-shop bags delivered to the concierge there. You don't even need to give a room number – he'll know who you are.

INTRODUCING MILAN

History

Turmoil and change have characterised Milan since Lombardy's earliest settlers decorated the walls of their caves with pictures of their hunting exploits. In the 5th century BC, Celts rampaged through, some staying to build the first settlement. Enter the Roman legions, quickly battering down the Celts' defences and establishing Mediolanum in 222 BC.

Celts and Romans slugged it out until the Second Punic War brought the Carthaginian, Hannibal, into the Po Valley from Spain. He knocked Roman heads together until he was sent packing. Then Mediolanum prospered in peace, exploiting minerals from the mountains and growing in influence until it was made capital of Rome's 11th region in 15 BC.

Christians were persecuted, but general peace lasted into the third century, when Milan became the power centre of the western Roman empires, surpassing even Rome. When Emperor Constantine gained control of the peninsula he recognised Christianity and ended persecution with the Edict of Milan in 313.

Bad times followed. Attila the Hun destroyed Milan in the 5th century, then in 539 the Goths destroyed it again. Charlemagne engulfed it in 774 and by 1000 the town was controlled by bishops. In 1045 the city threw them off and became a commune, leading to years of conflict with nearby city-states. It was incorporated into the Holy Roman Empire in 1162, when it was again razed.

Various powerful families fought to control it until 1450 when Francesco Sforza took over. The Sforza family ruled, apart from a few challenges, until 1535, when the Austrian Prince Philip took over. When he became King of Spain, Milan passed to Spanish control until 1706, when the Austrians reclaimed it.

HISTORY

Enter Napoleon. Seen as a liberator by Milanese chafing under Austrian rule, he was welcomed by most, and the Austrians bowed out. In 1805 Napoleon created the Kingdom of Italy in French-controlled areas, crowning himself King in the Duomo, with Milan as his capital.

When his fortunes shifted, Austria resumed control in 1815. Feeling the muscle of their booming industry, manufacturing and commerce, in 1848 Milan's citizens rose against the Austrians – the beginning of the Risorgimento – and liberated the city. The new republic lasted five months before it was defeated, but the city was freed by the entry of Victor Emmanuel's forces in 1859, when the new united Italy was born.

Dynamic growth continued, and Milan rightly styled itself as Italy's cultural and economic capital. It was partly to protect its manufacturing edge from labour unrest that Milan backed Mussolini in his rise. But by 1945 Milan was ready to move on, and rose against the occupying Nazis, liberating the city in just three days. Largely destroyed by World War II bombing, Milan was quickly rebuilt, and its hard-working population set about making it Italy's de facto capital. In the post-war boom, Milan led Italy from a quaint backwater to a major industrial nation. Milan today is the industrial, commercial, political, intellectual, design and fashion capital of Italy.

The government may be in Rome, but the power is where the money (and the stock market) is – in Milan. The city is all about innovation, whether it's in fashion, commerce or their commitment to the EU. Milan's history is all about today.

INTRODUCING MILAN

Lifestyle

Fashion and style are at the heart of the Milan lifestyle. Walk down any street and you can easily distinguish the locals from the tourists. Local men are in suits so well tailored that they might have been sprayed on. Perfectly knotted neckties are the finest silk, the

Fashion and style are the lifeblood of Milan

LIFESTYLE

latest width and the perfect colour. Shirt collars fit like kid gloves and shoes have the latest toe shape. And that's just the men. It has been joked that no woman in Milan would run to the corner shop for toothpaste without first applying her full makeup and doing her hair, but it's not so far from the truth.

Looks really do matter here, and if the clothes don't make the man, they at least tell everyone else what he's made of. It's not all snobbery and pretence. It's more an ingrained sense of style that's part of the air they breathe from childhood. It goes beyond clothes to architecture, home décor, even to the feel of a pen or keyboard. Whether it's a revolutionary building by architect Gio Ponti or the latest lemon-squeezer from Alessi, it will have class and style.

Italians are known for this sense of style, but the Milanese stand out even in Italy for their finely tuned perceptions, so it is not surprising that this overflows into the way they live. They dine out often and appreciate fine food, as well as its artistic presentation in smart surroundings. They are passionate about the opera, support artists and performers, and in general live the good life.

They are criticised by other Italians, especially those from the south, for their dour nose-to-the-grindstone behaviour, but these same regions are glad for the financial support that hard-working Milan's success brings to the general welfare of Italy. If the Milanese play hard, dress stylishly, dine well and furnish their homes elegantly, it is because they have earned the right.

And for all their *alta moda*, they are hospitable, helpful and friendly to visitors. Just join them in a bar after work or on a Saturday evening in Navigli and you won't see dour or buttoned-down. You'll see people having fun – people who know when to work and when (and how) to play.

INTRODUCING MILAN

Culture

Milan's artistic and musical heritage is a long and rich one. Important and influential Milanese, from cardinals and political leaders to giants of commerce, have supported arts and artists with commissions and left important legacies to the city in the form of buildings and art collections. Four of the city's five significant art museums are based on private collections, three of which are housed in buildings constructed by their collectors specifically to house them. It was the patronage of the Sforza family that brought Leonardo da Vinci and the Renaissance architect Bramante to Milan.

The Milanese continue this proud tradition by supporting contemporary artists. The Triennale's purpose is to encourage and recognise good design and two other major museums are dedicated to contemporary art. Milan's city-owned museums, including all the outstanding collections in the Castello Sforzesco, are free.

La Scala is, quite simply, the centre of the opera universe. Opera is popular with all ages and all classes of Italians, who consider it their national music. Don't be surprised to hear chic young Milanese – or the bus driver – humming bars from a Verdi or Puccini aria. La Scala's opening night – 7 December – is the highlight of the social season, and good seats for major performances are difficult to get any time.

It's not all classical and fine arts. Milan is the centre of the Italian music industry, with most major labels and several indies based there, and many big names in contemporary Italian music live in Milan as a result. A little-known venue where recording artists perform selections from their latest albums to smaller audiences

● *Teatro Dal Verme, Milan's other opera house*

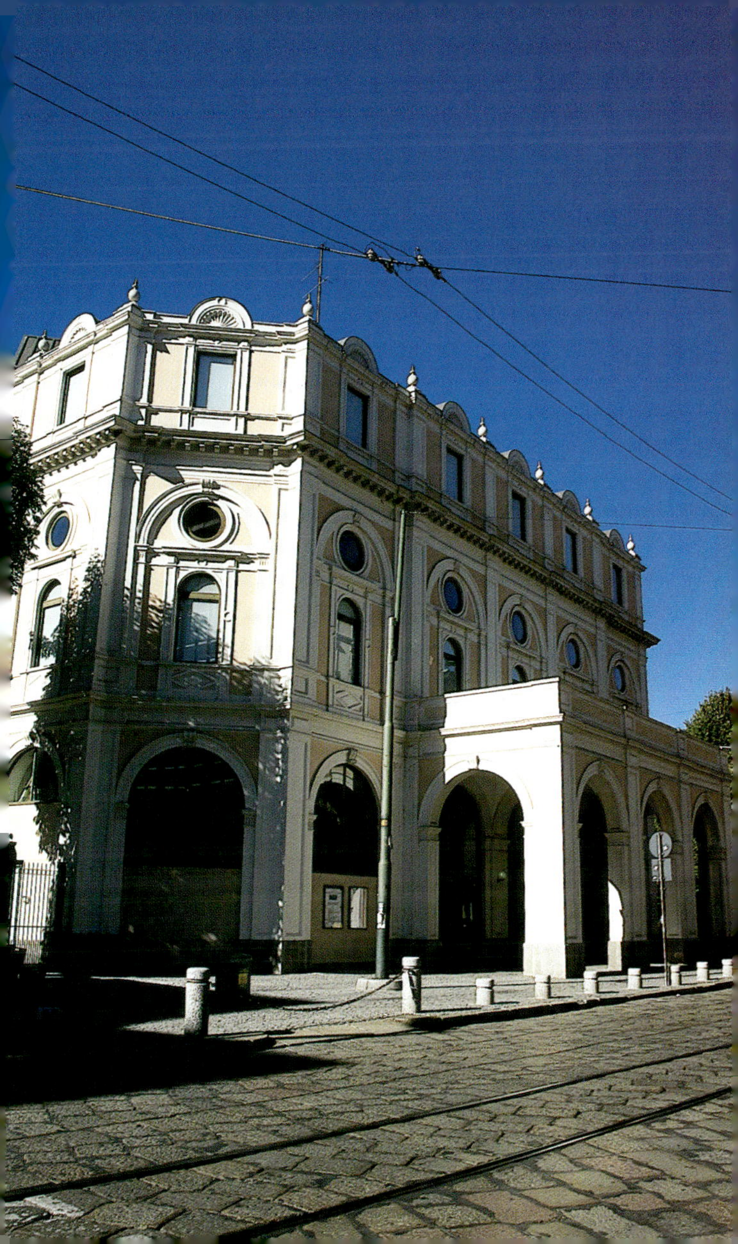

INTRODUCING MILAN

is the centrally located **Teatro Manzoni** (ⓐ Via Manzoni 42
ⓘ 02 7600 0231).

Concerts, whether Sunday morning jazz at Teatro Manzoni or a quartet playing chamber music at Teatro Dal Verme, are well attended. See Entertainment, page 28 for popular venues. The city's two primary classical and semi-classical performance ensembles are:

Orchestra Sinfonica di Milano Giuseppe Verdi

About 50 concerts are performed each season, most Thursday and Friday evenings and Sunday afternoons. Tickets are sold at the Auditorium, at the Tourist Office (ⓐ Piazza Duomo ⓘ 02 7252 4301) and online, where the full programme is also available.
ⓐ Auditorium di Milano, Corso San Gottardo (Navigli)
ⓘ 02 8338 9201 ⓦ www.orchestrasinfonica.milano.it ⓝ Tram: 3, 15

Filarmonica della Scala

The Philharmonic performs at Teatro alla Scala, with tickets starting at €5, available at the theatre or online. ⓐ Piazza della Scala
ⓘ 02 7200 3744 ⓦ www.teatroallascala.org ⓝ Metro: Duomo; Bus: 61; Tram: 1, 2

▶ *Motorcycles – Milan's popular mode of transport*

MAKING THE MOST OF
Milan

MAKING THE MOST OF MILAN

Shopping

Although it would be almost unthinkable to visit Milan and not at least walk through the Quadrilatero della Moda – the fashion quarter – few visitors actually shop there. First, the prices are absurd. Second, so are many of the clothes. These windows deliberately display the most outrageous new designs, which is what makes them so much fun to browse. Via Della Spiga offers the best.

Cut-price designer fashions are sold in the outlets and consignment shops, where you'll see overstocks, last season's line, items that have been worn by models and salesmen's samples. Discounts on these are usually 50 per cent to 70 per cent of the original tag. For more affordable clothes that still reflect that edgy Milano look, shop along Corso Buenos Aires or Via Torino or in the galleries off Corso Vittorio Emanuele. Most Milan stores are open 09.30–19.30 Tues–Sat, but smaller shops and those in outer neighbourhoods open 09.30–12.30 and 15.30–19.30, often closing Monday morning and opening only 15.30–19.30.

Street markets are fun to browse, and although they are filled with cheap imports, they can turn up some surprises, such as previously owned designer clothes for a few euros. A very popular one is on Tuesday and Saturday morning at Viale Papiniano, near the Porta Genova Metro stop. Milan has a full schedule of street markets, listed in the free newspaper *Hello Milano*.

Shows by craftspeople, where original works are sold by the makers, are quite a different thing, and are a good source of one-off works. These, like artisans' workshops and studios, give the added opportunity to meet the craftsman and perhaps watch works in progress. Every Saturday, **Fiera di Senigallia**, held along the Darsena, mixes original handcrafts with other items, new and used.

SHOPPING

For antiques and collectibles, try the shops behind Sant'Ambrosio or the Mercato dell'Antiquariato di Brera, where you'll find antiques, old books and jewellery on the third Saturday of every month. Markets at Naviglio Grande canal (last Sunday of each month), Piazza Diaz (last Saturday of each month) and Via Fiori Chiari in Montenapoleone (3rd Sunday of each month) also have antiques.

> **USEFUL SHOPPING PHRASES**
>
> **What time do the shops open/close?**
> A che ora aprono/chiudono i negozi?
> *Ah keh awra ahprawnaw/kewdawnaw ee nehgotsee?*
>
> **How much is this?**
> Quant' è?
> *Kwahnteh?*
>
> **Can I try this on?**
> Posso provarlo?
> *Pawssaw prawvarrlaw?*
>
> **My size is ...**
> La mia taglia è ...
> *Lah meeyah tahlyah eh ...*
>
> **I'll take this one, thank you.**
> Prenderò questo, grazie.
> *Prehndehroh kwestaw, grahtsyeh.*
>
> **Can you show me the one in the window/this one?**
> Può mostrarmi quello in vetrina/questo?
> *Pooh oh mawstrahrmee kwehllaw een vehtreenah/kwehstaw?*
>
> **This is too large/too small/too expensive.**
> Questo è troppo grande/troppo piccolo/troppo caro.
> *Kwestaw eh tropaw grahndeh/tropaw peekawlaw/ trawpaw kahraw.*

MAKING THE MOST OF MILAN

Eating & drinking

Some of Italy's top chefs work in Milan, and locals support them by dining out often, so the food scene is as fast-paced as the fashion *mondo modo*. But like any city, you can find really good, mediocre and inferior food, depending on where you look.

Travellers expecting the stereotypical Italian red-sauce-on-spaghetti may be surprised in Milan. While tomato-based sauces are found, Milanese cooking is more refined, and rice is as likely to be offered as pasta. In fact, perhaps the most classic of all northern Italian dishes is risotto Milanese, a dreamy-creamy rice dish made with saffron-infused broth and often incorporating porcini mushrooms, shellfish or other ingredients.

COUNTING EUROS

Food – and the social milieu of dining out – is a major part of the Italian experience, but it can be a pricey one. Quality is often – although not always – matched with high menu prices that equal those of Rome or Venice.

One euro-stretching strategy is to shop at markets, such as the daily one at Mercato Communale, for picnic ingredients (cheese, local salami and breads are always available) and carry them to Giardini Pubblici or Parco Sempione, or to the steps in Piazza Mercanti for an urban picnic.

If breakfast is not included with a room, cafés and bars are better value than hotels. Coffee with hot milk – *cappuccino* or *caffè latte* – is drunk only at breakfast. Coffee ordered at any other time of day will automatically be *espresso* unless you request *caffe americano*. In Italy, a bar is not just for alcoholic drinks; it's the place to go for a quick cup of coffee or a snack, too.

EATING & DRINKING

> **RESTAURANT CATEGORIES**
> The following price guide used throughout the book indicates the average price of a three-course meal (without drinks)
> **£** up to €25; **££** between €25 and €40; **£££** above €40

DECIPHERING THE NAMES

Italians call their eating places by a bewildering variety of names, and the lines between them blur. A trattoria usually has a more limited and less pricey menu than a ristorante, occasionally with a chalkboard list of choices. An *osteria* is supposedly a wine bar that serves snacks and sometimes a few dishes (think pub, Italian-style), but in practice an *osteria* may also be a chi-chi 'rustic' country inn. Likewise, a trattoria may be fancier than the neighbouring restaurant. Look at a menu, nearly always posted at the door, to be sure. A pizzeria is usually a full restaurant that specialises in wood-oven pizza, but it might also be a place that serves only pizza. For home-style cooking, look for signs advertising *cucina casalinga* and for a sandwich or quick lunch, go to a bar or café.

THE MENU

A typical menu will be divided into courses: *Antipasti* (starters), *Primi* (first course), *Secondi* (second course) and *Dolci* (pudding). Not all Italians order all four, and neither should you, unless you are very hungry. Vegetables are not usually served with the main dish; order them from the *Contorni* list.

Local specialities, along with risotto Milanese, include vitello (or cotoletta) Milanese, a breaded veal cutlet similar to Wiener schnitzel, and osso bucco – a tasty dish of slowly braised veal shanks in a rich tomato and wine sauce.

MAKING THE MOST OF MILAN

WINE WISE
Wine bars give you a chance to sample these by the glass without committing to a bottle. Look for the dry red Botticino and Cellatica, and the softer and more floral Gropello. Even in neighbourhood trattorie, the *vino di tavola* served by the carafe (*vino sfuso*, literally 'loose' or from the barrel) is almost certain to be very drinkable.

PRACTICAL DETAILS
Milanese dine late by northern European standards and many restaurants don't even open until 19.30 or 20.00. Lunch is served from 12.30 until 14.30 or 15.00. Select a spot for your evening meal early and book a table (or ask your hotel to do it). It is especially important to book ahead – at least a day or two – for popular restaurants on Friday and Saturday evenings.

◒ *Feast your eyes and your taste buds in a gelateria*

EATING & DRINKING

Many restaurants close on Monday and Tuesday, and in August, when the whole city seems to move to the lakes or sea, you may have trouble finding any eating places open at all.

In most city restaurants you can pay by credit card, although smaller *osterie* and trattorie may accept only cash. Tipping is appreciated, but is not a fixed amount. A 10 per cent tip is considered lavish; €2–€5 is a respectable tip, and a 20-cent tip is usually added at a bar. Larger upscale restaurants may add a service charge, which should be noted on the bill, and no further tip is expected.

> **USEFUL DINING PHRASES**
>
> **I would like a table for ... people.**
> Vorrei un tavolo per ... persone.
> *Vawrray oon tahvawlaw perr ... perrsawneh.*
>
> **Waiter/waitress!**
> Cameriere/cameriera!
> *Cahmehryereh/cahmehryera!*
>
> **May I have the bill, please?**
> Mi dà il conto, per favore?
> *Mee dah eel cawntaw, perr fahvawreh?*
>
> **Could I have it well-cooked/medium/rare please?**
> Potrei averlo ben cotto/mediamente cotto/poco cotto, per favore?
> *Pawtray ahvehrlaw behn cawtaw/mehdeeyahmehnteh cawtaw/pawcaw cawtaw perr fahvawreh?*
>
> **I am a vegetarian. Does this contain meat?**
> Sono vegetariano/vegetariana (fem.). Contiene carne?
> *Sawnaw vejetahreeahnaw/vejetahreeahnah).*
> *Contyehneh kahrneh?*

MAKING THE MOST OF MILAN

Entertainment & nightlife

High-brow, low-brow, club scene, student hangouts, funky, grand opera, drag shows, chamber music, grunge, cool jazz, Afro-pop, original language theatre, international celeb performances, street mimes, first-run cinema, underground bands – if it's entertainment, it's in Milan, proving that although they may work hard, they play just as hard.

The free *Hello Milano*, available at the tourist office, has a complete listing of shows, club nights, theatre schedules, concerts and performances at the major and minor venues. Ask also for *Milano Mese* which covers each calendar month. For what's on at clubs and at smaller and alternative venues, look for *Zero Due*, found in some cafés and bars.

CLUBS

It's true in nearly any city, but even more important in Milan that you need to know which night to go to which club. The music and vibe – and correspondingly, the clientele – change by the night of the week, so you need to know that on Saturday it's rock 'n' roll at Alcatraz, but strictly for the very young at Magazzini. Wednesday is student night at several nightspots and bars.

If you're not well dressed you'll be turned away. This is not true everywhere, but the smarter the club's clientele, the more likely the bouncer is to keep it that way. Just remember that you can't soar with the eagles if you dress like the turkeys.

Many clubs give you a card as you enter, which is punched at the coatroom and for every drink, then you pay as you leave. Admission charges, which range from €10–€20 may include one drink. At clubs all drinks – hard or soft – are usually the same price. Clubs are empty until near midnight, closing around 04.00. Most are closed in July and August.

The major international acts go to one of the three big entertainment venues. For tickets, go to a booking centre in one of the major music stores (the most centrally located is Messaggerie Musicali ⓐ Corso Vittorio Emanuele ⓘ 02 760 551), or from Ticket One (ⓦ www.ticketone.it), Easy Tickets (ⓦ www.easytickets.it) or BarleyArts (ⓘ 02 7611 3055 ⓦ www.barleyarts.it).

The major venues are:

Alcatraz
Big-name groups, usually Italian and European, such as Exodus and Nuclear Assault, have played here. ⓐ Via Valtellina 25 ⓘ 02 6901 6352

FilaForum
The most important venue for big-name international stars and groups – David Bowie, Placibo and the like. ⓐ Via G Di Vittorio, Assago (shuttle bus provided from the Metro) ⓘ 02 5300 6501

Magazzini Generali
Doubling as a dance club, the venue hosts a variety of travelling music shows. ⓐ Via Pietrasanta 14 ⓘ 02 5521 1313

● *Milan is the entertainment capital of northern Italy*

MAKING THE MOST OF MILAN

Sport & relaxation

Fitness has become the 21st-century obsession with the Milanese, threatening to overtake fashion. Health clubs are everywhere, so you can pump iron, tread, steam and be expertly kneaded almost on call. You'll want to be wearing the latest in work-out wear at most of these, of course – fitness hasn't completely overtaken fashion, just

● *Sailing on Lake Como*

SPORT & RELAXATION

given it a new outlet. Joggers have a hard time finding good routes, with only two in-town parks to choose from: Parco Sempione and Giardini Pubblici.

With the lakes and mountains so close, most outdoor sports enthusiasts head north to indulge their passions for hiking, climbing, sailing, windsurfing and paddle sports. Lakeside sports centres offer equipment rentals and hiking guides and maps are available at tourist offices (especially for trails around Lake Como). With so many mountains, there is a lot of territory to explore on mountain bikes; on Lake Como, rent from **Cavalcario Club** ⓐ Guello de Bellagio ⓘ 031 964 814

Boats of all sorts are available on the lakes. Ask for *barca* (boat), *barca a vela* (sailing boat), *motoscafo* (motorboat). Put these together with *noleggio* (for hire) and you're golden for the water. To swim, look for small *piscina* or *spiaggia* signs along the lake shores, but don't expect broad sandy beaches. Most are stony or made of gravel, so you will need a blanket or heavy towel.

GOLF

Lombardy has 35 nine- or eighteen-hole courses, nine promotional courses and nine practice locations, most open all year, so golfers should be happy either in the city or around the lakes. Be sure to call ahead for guest status and to reserve time.

Milan South: Golf Club Le Rovedine, 18 holes, par 72, only 4 km (2½ miles) from Milan ⓐ Via Karl Marx 18, Noverasco di Opera ⓘ 0257 606 420 ⓦ www.rovedine.com ⓒ Closed Mon

Milan North: Golf Club Milano, in Monza, has an 18-hole and a 9-hole course, par 72/36, 18 km (11 miles) from Milan ⓐ Via Mulini San Giorgio 7, Parco di Monza ⓘ 039 303 0812
ⓦ www.golfclubmilano.it ⓒ Closed Mon

MAKING THE MOST OF MILAN

Milan East: Molinetto Country Club is an 18-hole par 71 course, 10 km (6 miles) from Milan ⓐ Strada Statale Padana Superiore 11, Cernusco Sul Naviglio ⓣ 0292 105 128
ⓦ www.molinettocountryclub@virgilio.it ⓛ Closed Mon
West: Green Club Lainate, 18 holes, par 71, 10 km (6 miles) from Milan ⓐ Via A. Manzoni 45, Lainate ⓣ 0293 710 76 ⓦ www.golf-hotel.it
Lake Como: Golf Club Villa d'Este has an 18-hole course, among Europe's most challenging par 69 courses, 7 km (4 miles) from Como ⓐ Via per Cantu 13, Montorofano ⓣ 031 200 200 ⓦ www.villadeste.it
ⓛ Mar–Dec, closed Tues
Golf Club Mennagio e Cadenabbia: on the west side of the lake, is an 18-hole, par 70 course, 40 km (25 miles) from Como ⓐ Via Golf 12, Grandola ed Uniti ⓣ 0344 321 03 ⓦ www.mennagio.it ⓛ Mar–Nov

HORSE RIDING

Centro Ippico Tenuta la Torre welcomes all levels of riders, with English-speaking guides for trips into the hills and mountains around Lake Como. ⓐ Follow yellow signs between Menaggio and Porlezza ⓣ 0348 894 7 814 or 0348 008 0869 ⓝ Bus: line C12.
A 13th-century farm near Como offers rides around tiny Lake Montorfano. **Circolo Ippico Il Grillo** trips last from an hour to a full day and are offered at all levels of difficulty. ⓐ Via Chigollo 7, Capiago Intimiano ⓣ 031 462 219. English and Western saddles are available at both places.

FOOTBALL

Milano is home to two major football teams that use the same stadium. The **AC Milan** and **Inter** provide the Milanese with fierce rivalry that divides co-workers and neighbours twice a year, when they clash at their shared stadium in the San Siro district. Don't

SPORT & RELAXATION

even think about trying to buy tickets to those games. ⓐ Stadio Giuseppe Meazza, Via Piccolomini 4 west ⓣ 02 4042 432. Get tickets for AC Milan at ⓐ AC Milano Point, Via San Gottardo 2, Piazza XXIV Maggio ⓣ 02 8942 2711 ⓒ 10.00–19.30 Mon–Sat. For Inter tickets, go to ⓐ Ticket One/Spazio Oberdan, Viale Vittorio Veneto ⓣ 02 2953 6577 ⓒ 10.00–21.00 Tues–Sun

◓ *Why not visit the San Siro Stadium?*

MAKING THE MOST OF MILAN

Accommodation

It's not surprising that style-savvy Milan has some of Italy's classiest lodgings, from belle époque classics to the edgiest new art hotels. Surprisingly, the city also has a few of those charming small family-run inns that are more often associated with the lakes or Tuscany.

The distinctions can be puzzling. A hotel is usually exactly that – a building with guest rooms set along corridors, normally with a restaurant. Beyond that, designations are less clear. A small *albergo* (hotel) may resemble a *locanda*, although the latter is usually a nice country home turned into an inn. It's much better to go by the description and the size than by the classification.

Don't be surprised to find many small city hotels on upper floors of business buildings, with no ground-floor lobby – or hardly any lobby at all. These are often quite nice, and tend to be less costly than those with spacious public areas. Italy's star system helps you know what to expect of various lodging levels, and is based on regular inspections. Two-star hotels, for example, will have private bathrooms; 3-star will have in-room telephones and television. Internet points, oddly, may be available in the most modest hotel and unavailable in a costlier one.

The one thing that no star rating can tell you is whether the hotel is in an unsavoury neighbourhood, of which Milan has several. One of these, not entirely safe after dark, is around Stazione Centrale, but the many good hotels there are convenient for those

> **PRICE RATINGS**
> The following ratings indicate the average price of a room for two per night
> £ up to €100; ££ €100–€200; £££ over €200

ACCOMMODATION

arriving by train or air. Use taxis after dark here, especially if you have luggage.

Establish the rate when booking (always ask for special packages, especially on weekends, which can bring the most outrageous Milan rates down to reasonable), and request fax or email confirmation. Always have confirmed bookings for August around the lakes (Milan is nearly empty then), Easter week and for arrival and departure nights. Some lake hotels close November–March.

One way to be sure of a certain quality is to book rooms through affinity groups (different from hotel chains) such as Best Western, The Charming Hotels, Relais & Chateaux or SRS. Independently owned lodgings group together in these associations to pool their marketing efforts, but they also help travellers by assuring a level of standards. Their directories and websites have photographs and dependable descriptions.

HOTELS

Campeggio Citta di Milano £ Camping with wooded sites and 30 cabins available. ⓐ Via G. Airaghi 61 ⓘ 02 4820 0134 ⓕ 02 4826 2999 ⓦ www.campingmilano.it

Hotel Cavalieri della Corona £ The perfect choice for the last night if you're returning a rented car to Malpensa – or just to avoid last-minute hassles. Located in a nearby village, it has a pool, dining and free shuttle connections to Malpensa. ⓐ Via Baroldo 12, Cardano al Campo (Varese) ⓘ 0331 730 350 ⓕ 0331 730 348 ⓦ www.bestwestern.it

Hotel Del Sole £ This is a small but well-located hotel with clean and comfortable, if simply furnished, rooms. An attractive room accessed

MAKING THE MOST OF MILAN

by a spiral staircase serves as a breakfast room. ⓐ Via G. Spontini 6
ⓣ 02 2951 2971 ⓕ 02 2951 8689 ⓦ http://delsole.hotelsinmilan.it

Hotel London £ An amazingly well-priced hotel for the services offered. Clean and attractive, it has a 24-hour desk, air conditioning, TV, phones, room service, an attractive bar and lounge and more.
ⓐ Via Rovello 3 ⓣ 02 7202 0166 ⓕ 02 8057 037
ⓦ www.hotel-london-milan.com

Hotel Mediolanum £ Well located near the train station, Porta Venezia and Piazza Repubblica, it is modern and comfortable with in-room PC connections and on-site fitness facilities. ⓐ Via Mauro Macchi 1 (at Via Napo Torriani) ⓣ 02 6705 312 ⓕ 02 6698 1921
ⓦ www.mediolanumhotel.com

Hotel Sanpi Milano £ Close to the Stazione Centrale but in a safe neighbourhood, this hotel was recently renovated, with each room unique and featuring upscale décor with all expected amenities. A garden patio makes you forget you're in a city. ⓐ Via Lazzaro Palazzi 18 ⓣ 02 2951 3341 ⓕ 02 2940 2451 ⓦ www.hotelsanpimilano.it

Ostello Piro Rotta £ Rare Milan hostel quarters are in the vicinity of the Fiera. ⓐ Viale Salmoiraghi 1 ⓣ 02 3926 7095 ⓕ 02 3300 0191
ⓦ www.ostellionline.org

Hotel Gelsomina £–££ This 10-room hotel has recently been renovated, with bright and comfortable rooms, private baths, colour TV with high speed internet available, located near the Fiera and bus and tram lines. ⓐ Via Piero Della Francesca 4/7 ⓣ 02 3491 742
ⓕ 02 3180 1413 ⓦ www.hotelgelsomina.it

ACCOMMODATION

ADI Poliziano Fiera £–£££ A state-of-the-art business hotel near the Campione de Fiera, ADI is also close to other attractions, with all the expected gadgetry. ⓐ Via G. Carrisimi 26 ⓣ 06 852 101 ⓕ 06 8521 0210 ⓦ www.thecharminghotels.com

Antica Locanda Leonardo ££ Leonardo's *The Last Supper* is nearby in Santa Maria della Grazie. Rooms are a nice combination of traditional grace and modern comforts. ⓐ Corso Magenta 78 ⓣ 02 4801 4197 ⓕ 02 4801 9012 ⓦ www.leoloc.com

Best Western Hotel Felice Casati ££ Completely renovated within the past several years, the hotel is smartly comfortable and well located near Corso Buenos Aires. Check for special packages. ⓐ Via Felice Casati 18 ⓣ 02 2940 4208 ⓕ 02 2940 4618 ⓦ www.bestwestern.it

Hotel Gran Duca di York ££ It's hard to find better value in the centre of the city, than this small, well-kept hotel close to the Duomo and La Scala. ⓐ Via Moneta 1a ⓣ 02 874 863 ⓦ www.ducadiyork.com

▲ *Hotel Gran Duca di York*

MAKING THE MOST OF MILAN

Grand Hotel Verdi ££ Close to the hip Brera district, the Verdi plays on the operatic theme with dramatic stage-set décor. You could stage an opera in any of the huge guest rooms, and the supporting cast is helpful and friendly. Check the website for money-saving promotions that make this hotel even better value. ⓐ Via Melchiorre Gioia 6 ⓣ 02 62371 ⓦ www.grandhotelverdi.com

First Hotel Malpensa ££–£££ For morning departures, a room at the airport saves endless hassles, especially at this family-owned modern (built in 2001) hotel. Rooms are tech-wise and soundproofed and the free shuttles whisk guests off to their departure terminals. ⓐ Via F. Baracca 34, Case Nuove Somma Lombardo, Varese ⓣ 0331 717 045 ⓦ www.firsthotel.it

Hotel Pierre ££–£££ Very posh, well-located and equipped with wi-fi and sundry gadgetry, the rooms are a stylish mix of fine antiques and contemporary. Ask about special packages. ⓐ Via de Amicis 32 ⓣ 02 7200 0581 ⓕ 02 805 2157

ADI Doria Grand Hotel £££ Sumptuously appointed in contemporary modern style with overtones of art deco in the lobby and art nouveau in the café. All of the electronic connections are in-room. ⓐ Viale Andrea Doria 22 ⓣ 06 852 161 ⓕ 06 8521 0210 ⓦ www.thecharminghotels.com

Grand Hotel Duomo £££ The 162-room upscale hotel is right on Piazza Duomo in an 1860s *palazzo*, but bright and light, with décor in contemporary Italian high style. ⓐ Via San Raffaele 1 ⓣ 02 8833 ⓕ 02 8646 2027 ⓦ www.grandhotelduomo.com

ACCOMMODATION

Hotel Ariston £££ A modern and ecologically oriented hotel, close to the centre of town. Bicycles are available for guests, as is high-speed internet. ⓐ Largo Carrobbio 2 ⓣ 02 7200 0556 ⓕ 02 7200 0914 ⓦ www.hotelariosto.com/ariston/

Hotel De La Ville & La Villa £££ There are many reasons to stay in Monza, only half an hour from Milan, and this deluxe hotel is one of them. In addition to the first-rate rooms in the hotel there are the super luxurious quarters in La Villa, next door. ⓐ Viale Regina Margherita 15, Monza ⓣ 06 8521 01 ⓕ 06 8521 0201 ⓦ www.hoteldelaville.com

Hotel Spadari al Duomo £££ Truly an art hotel, the rooms and public spaces are hung with the best of contemporary Italian art, in striking colours and with all the required amenities. ⓐ Via Spadari 11 ⓣ 02 7200 2371 ⓕ 02 861 184 ⓦ www.spadarihotel.com

● *One of the elegant rooms at Hotel Gran Duca di York*

THE BEST OF MILAN

Whether you are on a flying visit to Milan, or taking a more leisurely break in northern Italy, the city offers some sights and experiences that should not be missed.

TOP 10 ATTRACTIONS

- **The Duomo** Italy's deep bow to Gothic (see page 60).

- **Duomo rooftop** If your stomach can stand it, this offers dizzying views to the Alps (see page 61).

- **Galleria Vittorio Emanuele II** The shopping arcade that is Milan's Living Room (see page 61).

- **San Ambrogio** Next to the Duomo, this is Milan's most significant church, with sixteen centuries of architecture (see page 92).

- ***The Last Supper*** One of the world's most famous paintings, found at Santa Maria delle Grazie (see page 79).

- **Quadrilatero della Moda** Three streets of fashionista nirvana (see page 63).

- **Castello Sforzesco** Now home to a number of manageable museums (see page 74).

- **Palazzo Bagatti-Valsecchi** A perfect palace for stepping into the Renaissance (see page 65).

- **Navigli nightlife** Hot, hip and hopping (see page 98).

- **La Brera neighbourhood** Chic, trendy and all that jazz (see page 82).

Bustle and posing in Piazza del Duomo

MAKING THE MOST OF MILAN

Your at-a-glance guide to seeing the best Milan has to offer, depending on how much time you have.

HALF-DAY: MILAN IN A HURRY

Do the Duomo, including the rooftop, even if it's the usual foggy day and you can't see all the way to the Alps. Then wander into Milan's favourite people-watching place, Galleria Vittorio Emanuele II to window shop and stop for an expensive coffee or aperitif at Zucca, a timeless café where locals meet. Go all the way through the galleria to Piazza alla Scalla, then to the last bit of medieval Milan, Piazza Mercanti. If it's time for lunch or dinner, the cosy Ristorante Mercanti is in the far corner.

1-DAY: TIME TO SEE A LITTLE MORE

After the Duomo and its neighbours, stroll up Corso Manzoni, stopping to look into one of the hidden gardens behind the buildings to your right, and into the Quadrilatero della Moda. The Palazzo Bagatti Valsecchi museum is in the middle of this district, a refreshing step back after you've seen your fill of the latest designer wear. Or, if Da Vinci interests you more than Versace, head for Santa Maria del Grazie to see *The Last Supper* (you'll have to get tickets in advance, see page 79), then continue on to the city's most historic church, San Ambrosio. By then it should be time for an aperitif at Café Sarducci, next door, where they offer a counter of generous snacks – a fine Milanese custom. For the evening, choose between the lively Brera's restaurants or the canalside Navigli's hip nightlife.

2–3 DAYS: SHORT CITY BREAK

Do whichever of the above you opted out of, then take in Castello Sforzesco, with at least a look into its museums to see

THE BEST OF MILAN

Michelangelo's last unfinished work, the *Rondanini Pietà*. Behind the castle is Parco Sempione, where you can go to the top of the Gio Ponte tower for a 360-degree view and take a break in the classy café below. While there, take in the latest design exhibit at Triennale, also in the park. If *The Last Supper* inspired you to know more about Da Vinci – or if things scientific and technical fascinate you – head for the Museo Nazionale delle Scienza e della Tecnica Leonardo da Vinci (National Museum of Science and Technology) to see his inventions and play with science toys in the interactive exhibits.

LONGER: ENJOYING MILAN TO THE FULL

After you've seen the sights of the city, do as the Romans did, and decamp to Lake Como. Even in the winter, the weather is milder there, especially in the Tremezzina Riviera on the western shore. In any other season, the gardens will be beautiful (they are green, even in the winter, but not open) and a variety of lake ferries provide cheap cruises. If you long for nightlife, stay in Como, the lake's largest town, a 40-minute train ride from Milan. Or choose the larger Lake Maggiore, favoured by a somewhat older crowd, but filled with activities and sights such as the Isole Borromeo (Borromeo Islands) with their palaces, gardens and mountain views.

MAKING THE MOST OF MILAN

Something for nothing

Milan, no matter how you measure it, is an expensive city to visit, but it is an economical one to see. Not only are nearly all the churches free (unlike Florence), with their own treasures of art and architecture to offer, but so are all the city-owned museums.

The entirety of the castle, Castello Sforzesco, is filled with treasures, and along with the must-see highlights, such as Michelangelo's *Rondanini Pietà*, gallery after gallery display far more than paintings and sculpture. The entire museum of practical and decorative arts shows how people once lived, what they wore, their furniture, even their musical instruments and armour. Arts in every medium, from iron to silk, spotlight the outstanding craftsmanship of the Middle Ages and Renaissance.

If your taste runs more to the contemporary, you'll find works of the Impressionists and Post-impressionist painters in the castle, too.

◆ *Admire Milan's magnificent Duomo for free*

SOMETHING FOR NOTHING

Or opt for the newly restored Villa Reale, facing Giardini Pubblici, just past the legendary Quadrilateral della Moda – itself worth browsing as a free 'museum' of contemporary art and culture. The villa, which was Napoleon's palace when he occupied Milan, has works by Gaugin, Van Gogh, Matisse, Cézanne and Picasso.

Explore ancient history, from the prehistoric through to the Roman city that Milan is built on top of, at the Civico Museo Archeologico (Archaelology Museum), where the only remaining parts of the Roman city walls and one of its towers have been excavated. Life didn't begin with the Romans, and prehistoric remains are not just shown, but interpreted so 21st-century visitors have a picture of how they lived. All free.

Jump ahead to the early 20th century and explore one of Italy's coolest cemeteries, an outdoor art gallery of art nouveau sculpture. Cimitero Monumentale, not far beyond Stazione Porta Garibaldi railway station, is hard to miss, with its oversized and uber-dramatic striped portico. You'll see some of the graceful bronze statuary before you even enter. If seeing this whets your appetite for more turn of the century design (called Stile Liberty here and art nouveau elsewhere) continue to wander in the streets nearby, looking for the distinctively decorated buildings.

Conclude your day with some free food, at one of the bars that indulges in the Milan 'happy hour' – happy indeed for customers, who can eat their fill for the price of one drink. If you don't find one handy, hop onto the green line Metro to the Caiazzo station and look for Art Factory (❷ Viale Andrea Doria 17 ❶ 02 669 4578 ❿ www.artfactory.it) just outside. Order a glass of a local wine and help yourself to dinner. If you arrive early enough, you might even get a table.

MAKING THE MOST OF MILAN

When it rains

A rainy day in Milan is the perfect time to indulge in either of two activities – or a bit of both. With a minimum of outdoor exposure, you can shop or you can nurture your sensitive cultural side and spend guilt-free time in art galleries without feeling as though you ought to be out ticking more sights off your list.

While shopping, you can even take a break at a pavement café and watch people go by, because Milan's 'main street' is indoors. Built in the middle of the 19th century, Galleria Vittorio Emanuele II was the largest shopping complex in Europe, and signalled the beginning of modern architecture in Italy. The Milanese still love it, and for many visitors its soaring glass dome and decorated shop fronts are their longest-lasting memory of the city. Watch the odd gyrations of people walking over the mosaic bull in the floor under the central dome, and try to catch one with your camera without being seen. They are hoping for a turn of good luck when they grind their heel into what would be the creature's tender parts, were these not made of stone.

From the elegant shops of the Galleria, make a dash across Piazza del Duomo to the cathedral itself, a one-stop culture/history fix that could keep you out of the rain for some time, especially if you splurge on the pricey ticket to see the treasury. Just counting the finger bones of saints takes a while, let alone admiring the exquisite gold work of the reliquaries they're stowed in. Nip downstairs from the front of the church and under Piazza del Duomo to see the palaeo-Christian baptistery excavated there. Save the roof for a better day – it's too slippery up there and you won't see anything in the rain.

WHEN IT RAINS

Besides, you can get an eye-to-eye view of it from the next shopping stop, La Rinascente. This is Italy's first department store. It takes its role in promoting Italian products and designers very seriously (there's an entire Alessi shop inside), and it's constantly redesigning its stores to stay on the cutting edge. The café on the top floor looks straight out at the Duomo rooftop. You can shop-hop under the arcades of Corso Vittorio Emanuele II to reach Galleria della Corso.

If you choose serious art over serious shopping, you could spend the good part of a day in the Ambrosina, just off Piazza del Duomo, or the lovely Museo Poldi Pezzoli, on nearby Via Manzoni.

● *You can't beat the Galleria for exercising your credit card*

MAKING THE MOST OF MILAN

On arrival

TIME DIFFERENCES
Italy is on Central European Time (CET). During Daylight Savings Time (late Mar–late Oct), clocks are set ahead one hour. Italy is one hour ahead of London, six hours ahead of New York and Toronto, seven ahead of Chicago, eight ahead of San Francisco and Vancouver, eight behind Sydney, twelve behind Wellington and the same as Johannesburg.

ARRIVING
By air
Visitors to Milan arrive at either one of Milan's two large airports – nearby Linate (❶ 02 7485 2200), used mostly for inter-Europe flights, and Malpensa (❶ 02 7485 2200), where most intercontinental traffic lands – or at nearby Bergamo, to which Ryanair has several flights from regional UK airports. Malpensa is 50 km (31 miles) from the city and halfway between Milan and Lake Maggiore, a handy starting place for visiting the lakes. Express buses connect Malpensa with the town of Como and several points along Lake Maggiore. Malpensa is connected to the city by Malpensa Express train (❶ 02 202 22) to Cadorna station and Malpensa Shuttle bus (❿ www.airpullman.com) to Centrale railway station. From Linate take No 73 bus to San Babila Metro or a shuttle bus to Centrale station. From the Orio al Serio airport at Bergamo there are regular bus connections to Centrale station. Tourist information, money exchange, ATM and car hire are all right at hand in either airport's arrivals area.

 Taxis wait outside the arrivals area, and are the best way to the nearby town of Gallarate, where trains connect to the west shore of

ON ARRIVAL

Lake Maggiore. A taxi is not the best way to get to Milan, since the buses take the same length of time, the trains less time, and either is considerably cheaper. However, if you do want to take a taxi, use only the yellow or white taxis lined up at the rank outside the terminal and never deal with people who come inside the terminal to tout rides.

By rail
Milan's Stazione Centrale railway station, where Eurostar and other trains (w www.trenitalia.it) from the rest of Europe arrive, is on the M3 (yellow) Metro line, four stops from the Duomo. Trains to lakes Como and Maggiore leave from this station, and buses from Malpensa and Bergamo airports arrive and leave from there. Taxis wait just outside the station; the minimum charge of about €3 increases at night, on holidays and for luggage. Taxis are the best way to get to your hotel after dark.

By bus
Buses arriving from long distances go to Piazza Castello. Although this terminus does not have as many services as the railway stations, it does have a taxi rank.

DRIVING IN MILAN
Unless you must, avoid driving in the city. Traffic is heavy and chaotic, and cars are not allowed to drive through the central area. You can drive in and out, but not through, as the city is divided into sectors. You cannot drive from one of these to another without first returning to the ring road and going around to the appropriate sector to enter the central streets again. Parking is difficult to find and expensive in car parks. Hotels charge extra, so it makes

MAKING THE MOST OF MILAN

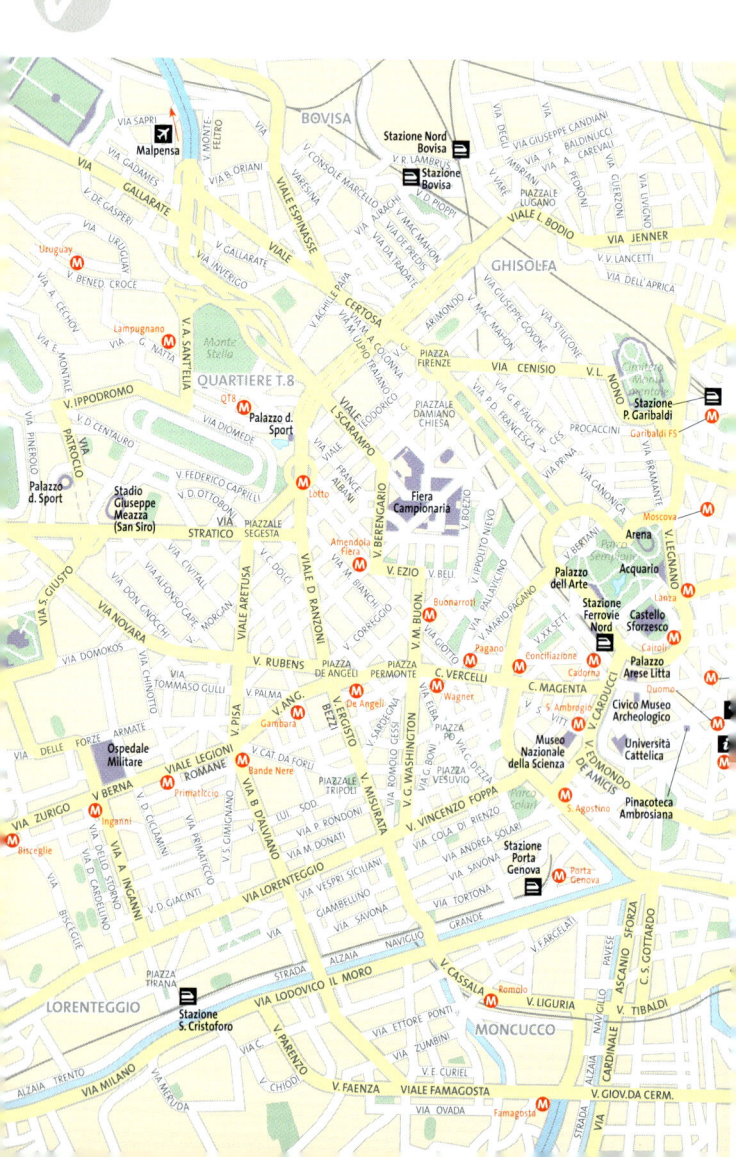

ON ARRIVAL

MAKING THE MOST OF MILAN

sense to pick up a rental car when you're ready to leave the city. For those visiting from the UK, remember, in Italy all traffic drives on the right.

FINDING YOUR FEET

No one has accused Milan of being a lovely or charming city – hurried post-World War II reconstruction concentrated on getting people and businesses housed, not on beautification. But its broad boulevards and lack of narrow medieval streets make it relatively easy to get around in.

You should always be aware of your surroundings in any city, and Milan is no exception. Avoid walking – especially alone – late at night in the areas around the railway stations or in parks or deserted areas. Women will be hassled less in Milan than farther south in Italy.

ORIENTATION

A look at a map shows how easy central Milan is to navigate. Piazza del Duomo forms a central hub from which avenues radiate, and most streets, while not in a strict grid, are straight and run in rows. Many of the major sights are close to Piazza del Duomo, so walking is the best way to explore them.

Plan your sightseeing to begin in the heart of the city, at Piazza del Duomo. Through the huge Galleria is Piazza della Scala and from these two squares radiate Corso Italia to the south, Corso V. Meravigla, becoming Corso Magenta, almost due west, and Via Alessandro Manzoni (which becomes Via Manin) heading northeast in the direction of Stazione Centrale railway station. These three avenues are the boundary lines for the three areas of the city described in this book.

ON ARRIVAL

GETTING AROUND
Public transport
ATM operates the Metro (Metropolitana), buses and trams and tickets are available at newsstands, bars, vending machines and at kiosks in some stations. You cannot pay on the bus or tram. Validate your ticket in the red meter as you enter the vehicle or go through the turnstyle. A ticket is valid for 75 minutes on unlimited trams and buses, but can be used once only on the Metro; you must use it first on the Metro, because tickets used first on a tram or bus are not valid on the Metro. If you plan to ride more than three times in a day, a better value is the day ticket (€3), which is validated only on the first use and can be used on any vehicle. A two-day ticket (€5.50) is even better value.

> **IF YOU GET LOST, TRY ...**
>
> **Excuse me, do you speak English?**
> Mi scusi, parla inglese?
> *Mee scoozee, parrla eenglehzeh?*
>
> **Excuse me, is this the right way to the old town/the city centre/the tourist office/the station/the bus station?**
> Mi scusi, è questa la strada per città vecchia/al centro città/l'ufficio informazioni turistiche/alla stazione ferroviaria/alla stazione degli autobus?
> *Mee scoozee, eh kwehstah lah strahda perr lah cheetta vehkyah/ahl chentraw cheetteh/looffeechaw eenforrmahtsyawnee tooreesteekeh/ahlla stahtsyawneh ferrawvyarya/ahlla stahtsyawneh delee ahootawboos?*

MAKING THE MOST OF MILAN

ON ARRIVAL

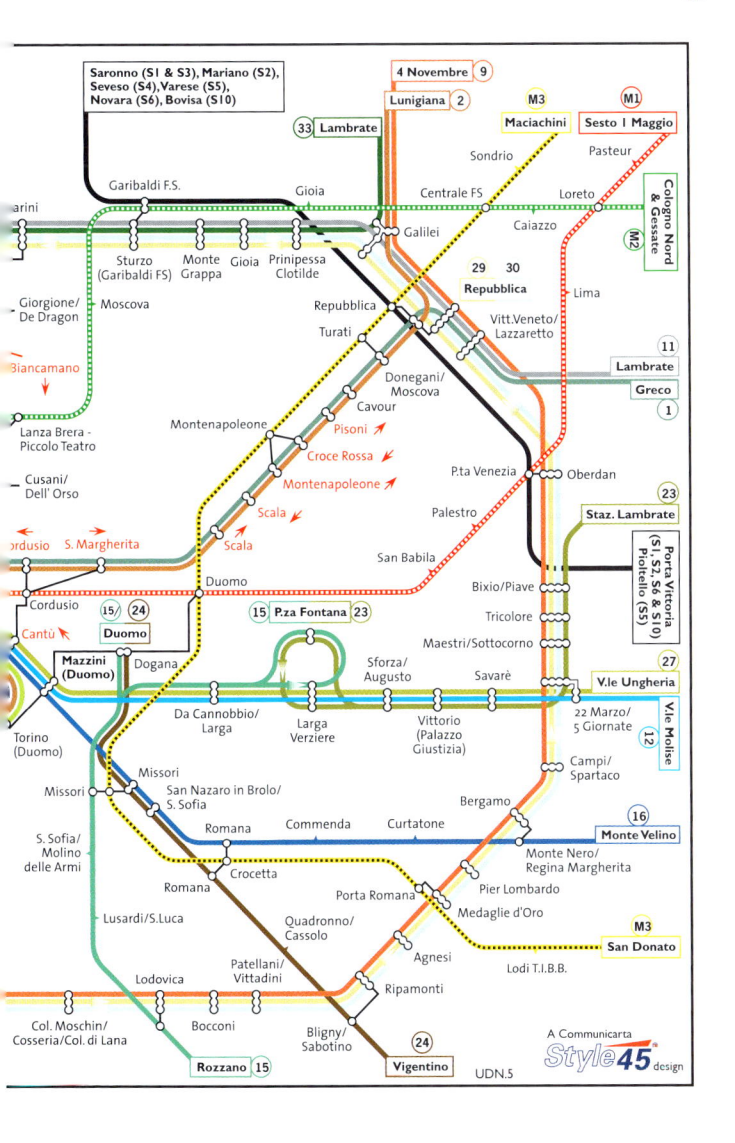

MAKING THE MOST OF MILAN

The Metro runs until only about midnight. After that, if no bus covers the route, you can use the Radiobus until 02.00 to get from the city centre to the outlying districts (❶ 02 4803 4803). Get information on all transit lines at the ATM office in the Duomo Metro station ❶ free phone 800 808 181 ❷ 07.45–20.15 Mon–Sat

Most major sights are on the CiaoMilano route, served by an old-style tram equipped with headphones and multi-language commentary. This hop-on-and-off service leaves from ❸ Piazza Castello daily at 11.00 & 13.00, plus Apr–Oct at 15.00 ❶ 02 7200 2584

Taxis are plentiful, but difficult to hail from the street. Go to the nearest taxi rank (look for a black and white sign), located at railway and bus stations, major *piazze* and larger hotels. Or you can telephone for one (❶ 02 4040 or 02 8585). All taxis are metered, with extra charges for luggage, night trips and if you call for a pick-up. Use only white taxis and do not use any touted by people inside stations.

CAR HIRE

While a car is more bother than it's worth in the city, it is the best (and in some places the only) way to explore the surrounding lakes. All major car hire agencies are at the arrivals halls of Malpensa, Linate and Bergamo airports. Among them is Auto Europe, which consistently offers some of the most competitive rates for Italy (❶ UK 0800 169 9797, Ireland 0800 558 892, USA 800 223 5555). For quick comparisons, visit ⓦ www.carrentals.com. Check rates before making your air reservations, because you can often do best with an airline's air-car package.

❶ *A detail from Casa degli Omenoni*

THE CITY OF
Milan

THE CITY

Piazza del Duomo & East

However you define the true soul of Milan – society, fashion, shopping, commerce, religion – you'll find it centred in this part of the city, between Piazza del Duomo and the enormous Stazione Centrale railway terminal, and stretching east to the suburbs.

SIGHTS & ATTRACTIONS

Major sights in eastern Milan cluster within a few minutes' walk, but do stray beyond the Duomo–Quadrilatero della Moda streets to find its quirkier reaches. Wander its streets to discover unsung churches with cool, quiet art-filled interiors and the more worldly pleasures of boutiques, cafés, bars and design houses.

Casa degli Omenoni
One of Milan's most startling buildings is this one, where stone giants lean out at street level to intimidate passers-by. The house was designed by the sculptor Leone Leoni in 1500. The interior is not open, but the exterior is enough!
ⓐ Via Degli Omenoni 3

Casa del Manzoni
The doorway and exterior of this author's home, just around the corner from Casa degli Omenoni, are elegantly decorated and worth a walk past. Manzoni's best-known work, *I Promessi Sposi* (The Promised Bride) is a must-read for Italian students.
ⓐ Via Morone 1 ⓒ 02 8646 0403 ⓒ 09.00–12.00, 14.00–18.00 Tues–Fri; admission free ⓜ Metro: Duomo

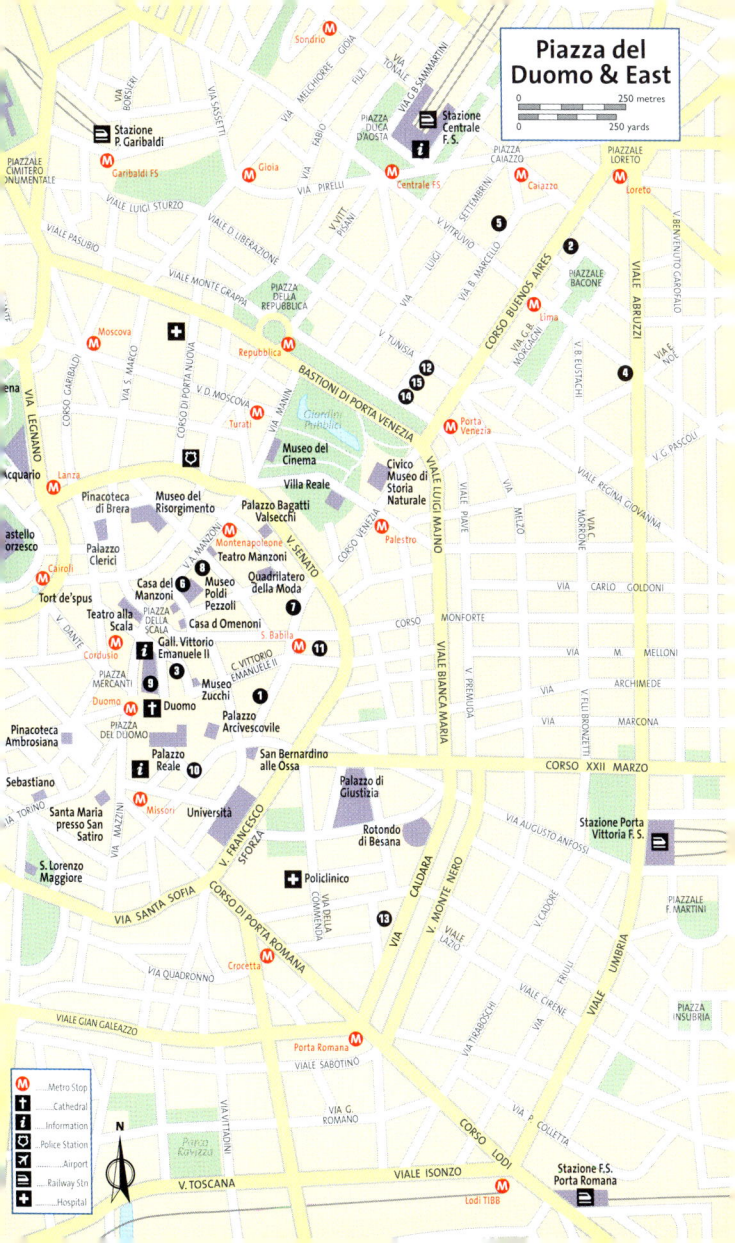

Piazza del Duomo & East

0 — 250 metres
0 — 250 yards

Map labels

- Stazione P. Garibaldi
- Garibaldi FS
- Sondrio
- Piazza Duca D'Aosta
- Stazione Centrale F.S.
- Piazzale Loreto
- Gioia
- Centrale FS
- Caiazzo
- Loreto
- Piazzale Cimitero Monumentale
- Viale Luigi Sturzo
- Viale Liberazione
- Via Pirelli
- Via Fabio Filzi
- Via Melchiorre Gioia
- Via Tonale
- Via G. B. Sammartini
- Via Sassetti
- Via Borsieri
- Viale Pasubio
- Viale Monte Grappa
- Via Vitruvio
- Piazza Caiazzo
- Via Settembrini
- Via B. Marcello
- Viale Tunisia
- Corso Buenos Aires
- Piazzale Bacone
- Lima
- Viale Abruzzi
- Viale Regina Giovanna
- Via G. B. Morgagni
- V. B. Eustachi
- Viale Noe
- Via G. Pascoli
- Via C. Morrone
- Moscova
- Piazza della Repubblica
- Repubblica
- Bastioni di Porta Venezia
- Porta Venezia
- Turati
- V. D. Moscova
- V. S. Marco
- Via Manin
- Giardini Pubblici
- Museo del Cinema
- Villa Reale
- Civico Museo di Storia Naturale
- Viale Piave
- Via Milzo
- Lanza
- Pinacoteca di Brera
- Museo del Risorgimento
- Palazzo Bagatti Valsecchi
- Palazzo Clerici
- Cairoli
- Tort de'spus
- Casa del Manzoni
- Museo Poldi Pezzoli
- Montenapoleone
- Teatro Manzoni
- Quadrilatero della Moda
- Palestro
- Corso Venezia
- Viale Luigi Majno
- Via Carlo Goldoni
- Teatro alla Scala
- Casa d'Omenoni
- Cordusio
- Piazza della Scala
- Gall. Vittorio Emanuele II
- S. Babila
- C. Vittorio Emanuele II
- Corso Monforte
- Viale Bianca Maria
- V. M. Melloni
- Via Archimede
- V. Flli Bronzetti
- Via Marcona
- Piazza Mercanti
- Museo Zucchi
- Duomo
- Piazza del Duomo
- Palazzo Arcivescovile
- Pinacoteca Ambrosiana
- Palazzo Reale
- San Bernardino alle Ossa
- Palazzo di Giustizia
- Corso XXII Marzo
- Sebastiano
- Santa Maria presso San Satiro
- Missori
- Università
- Rotondo di Besana
- Stazione Porta Vittoria F.S.
- Via Augusto Anfossi
- Piazzale F. Martini
- S. Lorenzo Maggiore
- Policlinico
- Via della Commenda
- V. Cadore
- V. Lazio
- Viale Umbria
- Piazza Insubria
- Via Santa Sofia
- Corso di Porta Romana
- V. Francesco Sforza
- V. Mazzini
- V. Monte Nero
- Via Caldara
- Via Tirabosschi
- Viale Cirene
- Crocetta
- Via Quadronno
- Viale Gian Galeazzo
- Porta Romana
- Viale Sabotino
- Via G. Romano
- Corso Lodi
- Via P. Colletta
- Stazione F.S. Porta Romana
- Lodi TIBB
- Piazza Vittorini
- V. Toscana
- Viale Isonzo

Legend

- M — Metro Stop
- Cathedral
- Information
- Police Station
- Airport
- Railway Stn
- Hospital

THE CITY

Duomo

The only way to take in the massive Duomo is to walk around it. Inside, a systematic walk around is a good idea. On the left side, in the north transept is one of the cathedral's greatest treasures, the Trivulzio Candelabra, a masterpiece of 12th-century goldsmithing depicting mythical creatures. Another highlight, behind the high altar, is the choir (🕒 13.30–17.00 Mon–Fri, 13.30–16.00 Sat) surrounded by deeply carved wooden panels.

ⓐ Piazza del Duomo ⓣ 02 8646 3456 🕒 07.00–18.45; admission free
Ⓜ Metro: Duomo; Bus: 50, 54; Tram: 1, 2, 3

▲ The vertiginous view from the Duomo

PIAZZA DEL DUOMO & EAST

Duomo, Basilica de S Tecla
Underneath Piazza del Duomo (accessed by a passageway inside the front of the Duomo), a palaeochristian baptistery has been excavated. Mosaics and patterned marble floors remain and glass cases hold stone carving and other artefacts.
ⓐ Piazza del Duomo ⓘ 02 8646 3456 ⓛ 09.30–17.00; admission charge Ⓝ Metro: Duomo; Bus: 50, 54; Tram: 1, 2, 3

Duomo, Le Terrazze (Roof)
Outside, on the south wall, is the entrance to the stairs and lift to the roof. Unless you suffer from terminal vertigo, do take this option. The view of the city – and the Alps if it's a clear day – is spectacular; but even better is the chance to get a saint's-eye-view of the cathedral itself, while standing amid the dozens of delicate stone spires that encrust it.
ⓛ 09.00–17.45 Mar–Oct; 09.00–16.15 Nov–Feb; admission charge Ⓝ Metro: Duomo; Bus: 50, 54; Tram: 1, 2, 3

Galleria Vittorio Emanuele II
'Il salotto di Milano' is what the locals call it: Milan's parlour. And although you'll pay dearly for a seat in one of its cafés, there's no better place in the city to watch the world go by. Once the largest shopping complex on the continent, this is Italy's first work of modern architecture. Shop or browse for silk ties, furs, gold jewellery or art books in impeccably turned-out shops, and stop to look – or aim your camera – straight up into its 48-m (157-ft) dome, even if you do feel like a tourist. Use the Galleria to get from Piazza del Duomo to Piazza della Scala.
ⓐ Piazza del Duomo ⓛ 24 hours; shops 09.30–13.00, 15.30–19.00 Mon–Sat Ⓝ Metro: Duomo; Bus 50, 54; Tram: 1, 2, 3

THE CITY

Giardini Pubblici (Public Gardens)
Green space is at a premium in Milan, so this grassy park within walking distance of Piazza del Duomo is a welcome break from stone and concrete. Villas and museums open onto its gardens, pools, fountains and playgrounds. Planetario Ulrico Hoepli (❶ 02 2953 1181) is open for planetarium shows and the free Civica Museo di Storio Naturale (Natural History Museum) is a favourite for children, with dinosaurs and realistic dioramas. The small Museo del Cinema in Palazzo Dugnani is crowded with examples of early film experiments, fascinating to cinema fans.

ⓐ Corso Venezia, Natural History Museum ❶ 02 8846 3280 ⓛ 09.00–18.00 Tues–Sun ⓐ Museo del Cinema ❶ 02 655 4977 ⓛ 15.00–18.30 Fri–Sun; admission charge ⓜ Metro: Palestro; Bus: 94; Tram: 1, 9, 29, 30

Teatro alla Scala (La Scala)
Open again, after what seemed like interminable restorations, the opera house is not just its old glorious self, it's a lot better. Carrara marble and elaborate chandeliers gleam from a thorough face-washing. Absorb the fascinating La Scala museum (below), or nip next door to the small church of S Guiseppe, on Via Verdi, a landmark in the history of architecture.

ⓐ Piazza della Scala ❶ 02 805 3418 ⓛ Open for performances, or through Museo La Scala ⓜ Metro: Duomo

Palazzo Reale
Facing the south side of the Duomo, beside the tourist office, this 18th-century pile was the palace of the Archduke of Austria in the late 1700s. Along with temporary art exhibitions, the palace houses the small Museo del Duomo.

PIAZZA DEL DUOMO & EAST

○ *Get away from the city's bustle in the Giardini Pubblici*

🅐 Piazza del Duomo 🅣 02 3932 2737 🅜 Metro: Duomo; Bus: 50, 54; Tram: 1, 2, 3

Quadrilatero della Moda (Fashion Quarter)
Lock your credit cards in the hotel safe before exploring the streets south of Piazza Cavour, enclosed by Via Montenapoleone, Via La Spiga, Via S Andrea and Via Manzoni to see window displays in the great fashion houses. 'Montenapo', as locals call this district, is

THE CITY

interspersed with beautiful old *palazzi* whose courtyards you can peek into – calming respites between the zany window displays.

San Bernardino alle Ossa

This baroque church alone is worth a glance, but the main attraction is the bizarre chapel to the right, its walls decorated in elaborate patterns of human skulls and assorted bones. Its beginnings were pretty straightforward: the neighbouring hospital's cemetery was over-full, and they built a small room to store the exhumed bones in the church. One thing led to another, and they became the décor.

ⓐ Piazza S Stefano ⓑ 07.30–12.00, 14.30–18.00 Mon–Fri, 07.30–12.00 Sat & Sun Ⓜ Metro: Duomo

CULTURE

Museo La Scala

Back in its old digs beside the theatre, the museum, too, has had a face-lift. Original designer sketches for costumes and stage sets join a touching display of the items on Verdi's desk at the time of his death.

ⓐ Largo Ghiringhelli 1, Piazza della Scala ⓣ 02 8879 2473
ⓑ 09.00–12.30, 13.30–17.30; admission charge, last entry 30 minutes before closing Ⓜ Metro: Duomo; Bus: 61; Tram: 1, 2

Museo Poldi Pezzoli

Fine arts are mixed with collections of everything from Lombard enamels to armour and textiles. Free audio-tours are available in English.

ⓐ Via Manzoni 12 ⓣ 02 794 889 ⓦ www.museopoldipezzoli.it

PIAZZA DEL DUOMO & EAST

🕒 10.00–18.00 Tues–Sun; admission charge, reduced Wed Ⓜ Metro: Montenapoleone

Museo Zucchi

A quirky little museum in the basement of the Zucchi store just off Piazza del Duomo displays thousands of hand-printing blocks, some dating from the 1700s.

📍 Via Ugo Foscolo 4 ☎ 02 9025 5230 🕒 15.30–19.00 Mon, 10.30–19.30 Tues–Sat; admission free Ⓜ Metro: Duomo; Bus: 50, 54; Tram: 1, 2, 3

Palazzo Bagatti Valsecchi

Almost a museum within a museum, this *palazzo* was the home of two 19th-century brothers who devoted much of their lives to building and furnishing it in the style of three centuries earlier. Signage, in English, describes the pieces themselves, which include tapestries, rare manuscripts, paintings by the Renaissance masters and a complete armoury. Step into the attractive courtyards, even if you don't visit the museum.

📍 Via S Spirito 10 ☎ 02 7600 6132 🕒 13.00–17.45 Tues–Sun, closed Aug; admission charge, reduced Wed, and good for a second day return if stamped Ⓜ Metro: Montenapoleone

Villa Reale

Reopened in 2006 after major restorations, Villa Reale once again glitters as it did when it was the residence of Napoleon and of the Italian kings. Amid its marble, stucco work and crystal chandeliers is a collection of 19th-century and early 20th-century art, including works by Gaugin, Van Gogh, Matisse, Cézanne and Picasso.

📍 Via Palestro 16 ☎ 02 7600 4275 🕒 09.00–17.30 Tues–Sun; admission free Ⓜ Metro: Palestro; Bus: 94

THE CITY

RETAIL THERAPY

You may require therapy (or resuscitation) after a spree in the rarified air of Milan's – and the world's – fashion central, the Quadrilatero della Moda. Close to the Quadrilatero, Corso Vittorio Emanuele is a traffic-free shopping zone between Piazza del Duomo and Piazza San Babila, with small covered galleries branching off to each side. Corso Buenos Aires is one of the largest shopping streets in Europe.

Belfe&Belfe Not just for climbers and hikers, B&B's leisure and sportswear is as durable as it is smart. ⓐ Via San Pietro all'Orto 7 ⓣ 02 781 023 ⓜ Metro: Duomo

Dolce & Gabbana Singer Madonna seeks out clothes by these two young designers, whose shop was designed by David Chipperfield. Look for vintage designs at Via Spiga 28, men's at Corso Venezia 15. ⓐ Via Spiga 2 ⓣ 02 7600 1155 ⓜ Metro: San Babila

I Santi An outlet at the factory, where you can see the leather goods made and buy cut-price. ⓐ Via B Corio 2 ⓣ 02 5416 981 ⓛ 08.30–12.30, 13.30–17.30 Mon–Fri ⓜ Metro: Porta Romana

Krizia The fashion designer that knocked staid Milan on one ear with the mini-skirt in the 1960s is still creating chic ahead-of-the-pack designs that appeal to young style-setters. ⓐ Via Spiga 23 ⓣ 02 7600 8429 ⓜ Metro: San Babila

La Rinascente Inside Italy's oldest department store is a collection of the latest and best of everything Italian, in a very stylish setting. Go

PIAZZA DEL DUOMO & EAST

to the top floor for the best views of the Duomo's spired rooftop, and to the 'bridge' for free internet access. ⓐ Piazza del Duomo ⓣ 02 885 2275 ⓛ 09.00–22.00 Mon–Sat, 10.00–22.00 Sun ⓜ Metro: Duomo

Le Firme A 4 Soldi Thousands of top-brand items are offered here at cut-price. ⓐ Galleria De Cristoforus 3 ⓣ 02 7601 8289 ⓜ Metro: San Babila

▲ *You may have to limit yourself to buying just a tie*

THE CITY

Prada Known as well outside Milan as here, Prada is possibly the most quintessential of all Milan names in fashion. Look for men's, sports and lingerie shops elsewhere in 'Montenapo'. ⓐ Via Monte Napoleone 8 ⓣ 02 7771 771 ⓝ Metro: Montenapoleone

Quadrilatero della Moda Not just for women, the showrooms and windows of the famed fashion houses show the most outrageous new designs in menswear, too. The prices are as astonishing as the clothes themselves. Most do not welcome obvious browsers, so dress the part and look interested if you plan to venture inside.

Te' Con Amiche Consignments of worn-once fashions and samples of top designer wear are sold at big discounts. ⓐ Via Visconte di Madrone 33 ⓣ 02 7733 1506 ⓝ Metro: San Babila

TAKING A BREAK

Ciao £ ❶ Cakes and sweets are the speciality of this café, not far from Piazza Fontana. ⓐ Corsa Europa 12 ⓝ Metro: Duomo

Spontini £ ❷ Order by the slice at Milan's favourite pizza joint and pay cash. It's been here half a century, between Corso Buenos Aires and Piazalle Bacone. ⓐ Via Spontini ⓣ 02 2047 444 ⓒ Closed Mon ⓝ Metro: Loreto

Agnello ££ ❸ Primarily pizza, but also known for risotto; you can get a full meal in this pizzeria right behind the Duomo or just a snack. ⓐ Via Agnello 8 ⓣ 02 8646 1656 ⓒ Closed Tues ⓝ Metro: Duomo; Bus: 50, 54; Tram: 1, 2, 3

PIAZZA DEL DUOMO & EAST

Bar Basso ££ ❹ Somehow, this bar east of Corso Buenos Aires has managed to stay popular through at least three generations; choose the speciality, a Negroni made with sparkling wine: Negroni sbagliato. ⓐ Via Plinio 29 ⓘ 02 2940 0580 ⓒ Wed–Mon ⓜ Metro: Lima

Frijenno Magnanno ££ ❺ Pizzas and calzone make up most of the menu at this casual place not far from Stazione Centrale. ⓐ Via Benedetto Marcello 93 ⓘ 02 2940 3654 ⓒ Closed Mon ⓜ Metro: Caiazzo

Café Dell'Opera £££ ❻ Expensive if you sit down at a table, but a very elegant place for *gelato* or pastry. ⓐ Via Manzoni 12 ⓘ 02 799 653 ⓜ Metro: Montenapoleone

● *You may be forced to give in to temptation in an elegant café*

THE CITY

Dolce & Gabbana Martini Bar £££ ❼ You might be sipping your apertif next to this year's supermodel in the bar of this menswear designer. Whoever is slouched in the leather seats next to you will be *alta moda* – and well aware of it. ⓐ Corso Venezia 15 ⓘ 02 7601 1154 ⓒ Closed Sun Ⓜ Metro: San Babila

Emporio Armani Café £££ ❽ Everything is stylish, from the building and décor to the people who shop in this Armani complex. ⓐ Via Manzoni 31 ⓘ 02 7231 8680 ⓒ Closed Sun Ⓜ Metro: Montenapoleone

Zucca £££ ❾ As stylish now as it was when Verdi met fellow musicians at its tables, this art deco landmark at the Galleria is the place for an apertif. ⓐ Piazza del Duomo 21 ⓘ 02 8646 4435 Ⓜ Metro: Duomo; Bus: 50, 54; Tram: 1, 2, 3

AFTER DARK

Italy's only gay street, Via Sammartini, next to Stazione Centrale, has more than its share of nightlife and Corso Vittorio Emanuele II has the city's densest concentration of cinemas. The Ripamonte district, beyond the Romano railway station, has a growing number of music venues, including the 900-seat Magazzini Generali.

Restaurants

Giardino di Giada £ ❿ So maybe you didn't come to Italy to eat Chinese food, but it's cheap, good and handy; close to the Duomo. ⓐ Via Palazzo Reale 5 ⓘ 02 8053 891 ⓒ Tues–Sun Ⓜ Metro: Duomo; Bus: 50, 54; Tram: 1, 2, 3

PIAZZA DEL DUOMO & EAST

Brek £–££ ⓫ Healthy salads, grilled meat, fresh cooked mains. Unlike others in this small chain of wholesome, bright restaurants, this one has table service. ⓐ Piazzetta Giordano 1 ⓘ 02 7602 3379 ⓜ Metro: San Babila

Da Ilia ££ ⓬ A neighbourhood institution near the Giardini Pubblici (Public Garden). ⓐ Via Lecco 1 ⓘ 02 2952 1895 ⓦ www.ristorante-ilia.it ⓜ Metro: Porta Venezia

Il Sole ££ ⓭ A wine bar long before they were hot, Il Sole serves full meals of Mediterranean dishes and wine by the glass. ⓐ Via Curtatone 5 ⓛ Mon–Sat, closed Sat lunch ⓘ 02 5518 8500 ⓜ Metro: Crocetta

Trattoria Il Carpaccio ££ ⓮ Small-town value, big-city quality in a friendly neighbourhood trattoria. As the name suggests, the carpaccio is excellent, and so is the tortelloni. ⓐ Via Palazzi 9 (opposite Hotel Sanpi) ⓘ 02 2940 5982 ⓜ Metro: Porta Venezia

Joia £££ ⓯ Vegans and vegetarians at last have a top-class Milanese restaurant that caters to them with imaginative dishes – and won a Michelin star for it. ⓐ Via Castaldi 18 ⓘ 02 2952 2124 ⓦ www.joia.it ⓛ Mon–Sat, closed Sat lunch and Aug ⓜ Metro: Repubblica; Tram: 29

Cinemas & theatres
Corso Vittorio Emanuele II, between the Duomo and Piazza San Babila, is Cinema Alley, with not only the most theatres but the biggest of them.

THE CITY

Spazio Oberdan Long closed and recently refurbished as a Cineteca, or film library, this classic old movie house is again showing rare vintage flicks. ⓐ Viale Vittorio Veneto 2 ⓣ 02 7740 6300 ⓦ www.cinetecamilano.it Ⓜ Metro: Porta Venizia; Tram: 29

Teatro alla Scala To perform at La Scala is the life goal of any opera singer. To get a ticket for a good seat is the goal of opera-lovers. To be there on opening night, 7 December, is the right of anyone who's anyone in Milan society. Along with the opera, the philharmonic orchestra, Filarmonica della Scala, performs at La Scala. Tickets for the latter run as low as €5, opera tickets are €10–€170; the lower the price, the higher the seat, and the upper balconies are a dizzying distance and pitch above the stage. ⓐ Piazza della Scala ⓣ 02 7200 3744 ⓦ www.teatroallascala.org Ⓜ Metro: Duomo; Bus: 61; Tram: 1, 2

Teatro Manzoni Along with evening performances of artists singing selections from their latest albums, Teatro Manzoni offers Sunday morning Apertivo in Concerto jazz concerts. Buy a ticket in advance, arrive at 10.00, wait an hour and scramble for a seat. ⓐ Via Manzoni 42 ⓣ 02 763 6901 ⓦ www.teatromanzoni.it Ⓜ Metro: Montenapoleone; Bus: 61; Tram: 1, 2, 20

Bars, clubs & discos
Afterline Popular gay disco with theme nights, but anyone is welcome here and in most other gay clubs on this street. ⓐ Via Sammartini 25 ⓣ 02 669 2130 Ⓜ Metro: Centrale FS

G Lounge A name-brand local DJ spins dance discs for a smart clientele from the fashion district. ⓐ Via Larga 8 ⓣ 02 805 3042 Ⓜ Metro: Duomo

PIAZZA DEL DUOMO & EAST

Jumpin' Jazz Ballroom Live jazz for Saturday night dancing makes this worth the trip to the burbs for jazz fans. ❸ Viale Monza 140 ❶ 334 311 2926 ⓦ www.jumpinjazz.it ❶ Sat ❻ Taxi or Radiobus until 02.00

La Salumeria della Musica Cabaret and live music (including jazz) bring a young crowd to this old Ripamonti factory. ❸ Via Pasinetti 2 ❶ 02 5680 7350 ⓦ www.lasalumeriadellamusica.com ❶ 21.00–01.00 Mon–Sat ❻ Bus: 95; Tram: 24

Magazzini Generali International acts on tour play here to a 900-seat audience and it's popular for club nights. Free Wednesdays draw students, Friday is house music with a largely gay crowd. ❸ Via Pietrasanta 14 (Ripamonti) ❶ 02 5521 1313 ❶ 23.30–04.00 Wed, Fri–Sat, closed July, Aug ❻ Taxi from Porta Romana railway station

Plastic Leave yours at home (they take only cash), and take care how you dress, or even the hefty admission fee won't get you into the trendiest of the trendy. The beat is house and hip hop. ❸ Viale Umbria 120 ❶ 02 733 996 ❶ 24.00–05.00 Thur–Sat, 20.00–02.00 Sun, closed July, Aug ❻ Bus: 92

Rocket Alternative DJs spin rock, electro and after shows you'll find indie artists playing here when they are in town. Free admission makes it rare, and popular. ❸ Via Pezzotti 52 (Western Ripamonti) ❶ 02 8950 3509 ⓦ www.therocket.it ❶ 23.00–03.00, closed Aug ❻ Tram: 3, 15; Bus: 65, 91

THE CITY

Castello Sforzesco & Northwest Milan

From the tight-packed little streets of Brera to the open green spaces of Parco Sempione, the northwest neighbourhoods of Milan are filled with variety – and surprises. No one would guess, for example, that Brera's close-packed buildings hide a lush botanic garden. This is a part of the city worth exploring on foot, since its main sights are all within walking distance.

SIGHTS & ATTRACTIONS

The Sforza Castle is the centrepiece of this northern quarter, a fortified palace inside a walled enclosure. From inside its walls the Visconti and the Sforza families ruled much of northern Italy from the Middle Ages until 1500. Beyond it stretches one of Milan's only two inner-city green spaces.

Castello Sforzesco

Now home to a clutch of museums, Castello Sforzesco was begun in the 1360s and work continued for a century. Wander inside even if the museums are closed. There are some interesting things to see inside – frescoes in the loggia of the Corte Ducale (Dukes' Court) and a display of ornamental stone carving – and it's free. Because of ongoing renovations, some of the galleries or collections may be closed; see the helpful booklet *MilanoMusei*, from the Tourist Office for updates.

ⓐ Piazza Castello ⓑ Castle grounds open 08.00–20.00; admission free Ⓜ Metro: Cadorna or Cairoli

Castello Sforzesco & Northwest Milan

THE CITY

Cimitero Monumentale
Although a few greats are buried here – conductor Arturo Toscanini, poet Salvatore Quasimodo and author Alessandro Manzoni among them – the reason for going here is to see the amazing tombs. The entrance is impressive enough, but inside, the monuments that mark the final resting places of the once rich and famous are many in the art nouveau style – called Stile Liberty here. A map, in English, leads to some of the best, many by noted Italian sculptors.
ⓐ Piazzale Cimitero Monumentale (north of Stazione Porta Garibaldi) ⓘ 02 659 9938 ⓒ 08.30–17.15 Tues–Fri, 08.30–17.45 Sat & Sun; admission free Ⓝ Tram: 3, 4

▲ *You don't see many cemeteries as stylish as Cimitero Monumentale*

Orto Botanico di Brera

An astonishing variety of plant species, including Europe's oldest ginkgo tree, are hidden in the inner courtyard of the huge Brera museum and art school, without an outer clue of their existence. Enter a quiet green oasis with moody stonework accents, all walled by surrounding buildings.

ⓐ Via Brera 28 ⓣ 02 8901 0419 ⓦ www.horti.unimore.it
ⓗ 09.00–12.00, 13.00–16.00 Mon–Fri; admission free Ⓜ Metro: Lanza or Montenapoleone

Palazzo dell'Arte (Triennale)

The building, constructed to house the premier Italian design show every third year, works well as a showcase for art and design. Inside there are always high-level shows and exhibitions, often international in scope.

ⓐ Viale Alemagna 6 (in Parco Sempione) ⓣ 02 7243 4208
ⓦ www.triennale.it (tickets at biglietteria@triennale.it)
ⓗ Hours vary with current show; admission charge Ⓜ Metro: Cadorna Triennale

Parco Sempione

Along with the Triennale, the leafy expanses of this rare patch of green in central Milan can't quite hide the strange Torre Branco. The English-style park is a good place to rest your eyes after they've overdosed on stone and architecture, and to wander the curving pathways. If you like art nouveau, be sure to see the fanciful aquarium pavilion at the Via Gadio edge of the park.

ⓐ Between Castello and Corso Sempione ⓗ 06.30–21.00, later spring and summer; admission free Ⓜ Metro: Cadorna; Tram: 1, 3, 4

THE CITY

Torre Branco
Designed by famed architect Gio Ponte and his associates, the tower was built to celebrate the 1933 Triennale art exhibition. Closed since the early 1970s, a rush of money from Milanese distillers, Fratelli Branca, completely restored it. The view of Milan and the Alps, if the day is clear, is worth the three euros. There's a stylish café at the base.
ⓐ Viale Camoens ⏰ 10.30–12.30, 16.00–18.30 Wed, 10.30–13.00, 15.00–18.30 and 20.30–24.00 Sat; 10.30–14.00, 14.30–19.00 Sun; admission charge Ⓜ Metro: Cadorna; Tram: 1, 3, 4

▲ *One of the tombs at the Cimitero Monumentale*

CASTELLO SFORZESCO & NORTHWEST MILAN

Santa Maria delle Grazie

Although nearly everyone comes here to see one of the world's most famous paintings, *The Last Supper*, in the adjoining monastery, the church itself has some interesting things to see. The architect Bramante gave the 15th-century Gothic church a make-over, with a new face, a rebuilt sanctuary and the delightful little 'Frog Cloister' behind the church. Inside, in the second chapel on the right, a Caravaggio painting (a treasure in its own right) stands in for the Titian stolen by Napoleon's army in 1797 and taken off to the Louvre, from which it has never been returned.

You'll need to reserve well in advance to look inside the Cenacolo Vinciano, at Leonardo da Vinci's *The Last Supper*. The painting's fresco base began to deteriorate soon after da Vinci finished it, then the building was bombed in World War II and the painting stood for several years open to the weather. It has been restored by the best in the business, but it shows its age and the tough life it has led. Do make the effort to see it – it's considered one of the great masterpieces of Western art.

ⓐ Piazza Santa Maria delle Grazie ⓘ 02 8942 1146 ⓒ Church open 07.00–12.00, 15.00–19.00, Cenacolo 08.15–18.45 Tues–Sun; admission charge ⓘ Timed Cenacolo tickets must be reserved in advance; operators speak English ⓜ Metro: Conciliazione

Tort de' spus (Wedding Cake Fountain)

One of the prettiest fountains in Italy stands in front of Castello Sforzesco, rising and falling in a great while circle of bubbling water, hence its local name. It's a favourite place to meet, to sit and just to admire.

ⓐ Piazza Castello ⓜ Metro: Cairoli

THE CITY

◓ *Cool off by the Wedding Cake Fountain*

CULTURE

Civico Museo Archeologico (Archaelology Museum)

The highlights of the museum are its Roman works, including a 24-sided Roman tower, Torre Ansperto. There's a lot more of the ancient world in the museum, which also includes the church of San Maurizio itself, where you can see the excellent frescoes by

CASTELLO SFORZESCO & NORTHWEST MILAN

Bernardo Luini and his sons that almost completely cover the interior in vivid colours.

ⓐ Corso Magenta 15 ⓘ 02 8645 0011 ⓒ 09.30–17.30 Tues–Sun. Church open 09.00–12.00, 14.00–17.30 Tues–Sun; admission free Ⓝ Metro: Cadorna

Civiche Raccolte d'Arte Antica del Castello (Art Museum)

The arrangement of the many different art museums inside the castle may vary with renovations, but the collections remain the same – and are pretty remarkable. Most outstanding – and enough reason for a visit – is Michelangelo's enormously moving *Rondanini Pietà*. The artist was working on it within a few days of his death at age 88. From medieval stone and wood carvings to one of Europe's best collections of 20th-century art, featuring Picasso and his contemporaries, this museum has something for everyone.

ⓐ Castello Sforzesco, Piazza Castello ⓘ 02 861 125 ⓒ 09.00–17.30 Tues–Sun; admission free Ⓝ Metro: Cadorna or Cairoli

Civiche Raccolte di Arte Applicata (Decorative Arts Museum)

See how the upper half (more like the upper five per cent) lived in the glory days of the Renaissance, by admiring their furniture (a mind-boggling collection), textiles, clothing, jewellery and home decorations. Collections of armour, weapons and musical instruments are also in this museum, as well as the 12 Trivulzio tapestries that surround one of the music collection galleries. These are considered the most important masterpieces of Renaissance textiles.

ⓐ Castello Sforzesco, Piazza Castello ⓘ 02 861 125 ⓒ 09.00–17.30 Tues–Sun; admission free Ⓝ Metro: Cadorna or Cairoli

THE CITY

Pinacoteca di Brera (Brera Art Museum)
All the great Italian painters are represented in the massive collection here, the largest in the city: Titian, Raphael, Caravaggio, Tintoretto, Veronese, Luini, Tiepolo, Canaletto.
ⓐ Via Brera 28 ⓣ 02 722 631 ⓦ www.brera.beniculturali.it
🕒 08.30–19.15 Tues–Sun; may vary Ⓜ Metro: Lanza or Montenapoleone

RETAIL THERAPY

Antiques shops have begun to join the clothing, accessory and gift boutiques in the narrow streets near Pinacoteca di Brera, once the Bohemian quarter of art students and intellectuals. Beyond Parco Sempione, Corso Vercelli has some department stores; check Via Belfiore, off Corso Vercelli, for shoes. Via Canonica, in the Paolo Sarpi area, Milan's former Chinatown, has a lot of leather shops and nearby are iron, glass, wood and other crafts studios.

Accornero For *fashionista* homes, this is the stop for stylish décor and accessories. ⓐ Via Ponte Vetro 17 (just off Piazza del Carmine) ⓣ 02 8909 6297 Ⓜ Metro: Cairoli

Atribu Young designers show their latest at this shop. You may get a piece by tomorrow's Versace or Gucci. ⓐ Corso Garibaldi 40 ⓣ 02 867 127 Ⓜ Metro: Lanza

La Piccola Legatoria Beautifully bound notebooks and paper-covered boxes in lively colours and smart designs make easy-to-carry-home gifts – and you can even buy the paper for gift-wrapping. ⓐ Via Palermo 11 ⓣ 02 861 113 ⓦ www.lapiccolalegatoria.it Ⓜ Metro: Lanza

CASTELLO SFORZESCO & NORTHWEST MILAN

◆ *Castello Sforzesco*

Luca Even if you don't need shoes, look into this shop to see its lux marble interior. ⓐ Corso Vercelli 11 ⓣ 02 4800 8010
Ⓜ Metro: Conciliazione

Melegari Hats, hats, hats – most with veils – have made this shop a must-stop for the chic since 1914. Men's hats, as well, plus ties, belts and gloves. ⓐ Via Paolo Sarpi 19 ⓣ 02 312 094
Ⓜ Metro: Moscova

THE CITY

Meru Not fine jewels, but costume jewellery made of less costly materials decorated with precious metals. Not your usual bijou.
ⓐ Via Solferino 3 ⓣ 02 8646 0700

10 Corso Como Not the ultra pricey main store, but a cut-price outlet on the lower-rent street between Stazione Porta Garibaldi and Cimiterio Monumentale. The same high-style for men and women, but it's last season's. ⓐ Via Tazzoli 3 ⓣ 02 2901 5130 ⓐ Wed–Sun afternoons Ⓜ Metro: Garibaldi FS; Tram: 3, 4, 11; Bus: 41

TAKING A BREAK

Cafés and little bars with sandwiches are plentiful, especially in the shopping streets of Brera and around Corso Vercelli. Less glitzy than those closer to Piazza del Duomo, but still a good mix of styles.

Grand'Italia £ ❶ Pizza in a pleasant busy Brera atmosphere.
ⓐ Via Palermo 5 ⓣ 02 877 759 ⓒ Wed–Mon Ⓜ Metro: Moscova

El Tumbun de San Marc £ ❷ Stop for a beer at this Brera landmark that survived the upscaling of the neighbourhood. ⓐ Via San Marco 20 ⓣ 02 659 9507 ⓒ Mon–Sat Ⓜ Metro: Moscova

Fabbrica £–££ ❸ Good pizzas, some mains, good desserts.
ⓐ Viale Pasubio 2 ⓣ 02 655 2771 ⓒ Tues–Sun Ⓜ Metro: Garibaldi FS

Corso Como Café ££–£££ ❹ Stop in at the *alta moda* complex of Corso Como10, at least to have coffee or a cocktail in Carla Sozzani's courtyard café. Be sure you're well dressed, or all the tables may be reserved. ⓐ Corso Como 10 ⓣ 02 653 531 Ⓜ Metro: Garibaldi FS

CASTELLO SFORZESCO & NORTHWEST MILAN

Just Cavalli Café £££ ❺   Prime real estate, at the foot of the Torre Branco, by a prime name in fashion. Food as well as drink, served at some of the city's few tree-surrounded tables. ⓐ Viale Camoens ⓘ 02 311 817 ⓛ 20.00–02.00 Mon–Sat, 12.30–16.00 Sun Ⓜ Metro: Cadorna; Tram: 1, 3, 4

AFTER DARK

Some of the hottest nightclubs are in the streets near the Castello, and restaurants hide on the small streets off the major avenues. Meet people and have a good inexpensive meal, at **Old Fashion Café** ⓐ International Place, Viale Alemagna 6 ⓘ 02 8056 231 ⓦ www.oldfashion.it ⓛ 20.00 each Wednesday

Restaurants

Casa Fontana ££ ❻   Risotto Milanese is the city's signature dish, and you won't find it in more varieties anywhere else. Here it is offered in more than 20 variations. ⓐ Piazza Carbonari 5 ⓘ 02 670 4710 ⓛ Tues–Sat (no lunch Sat) Ⓜ Metro: Sondrio

Pizzeria di Porta Garibaldi ££ ❼   Handmade *gnocchi* (potato dumplings) and crusty pizza, available by the slice, make this a good choice for day or evening. ⓐ Corso Como 6 ⓘ 02 655 1926 Ⓜ Metro: Garibaldi FS

Trattoria C'era Una Volta ££ ❽   The trattoria serves traditional osso bucco in a non-touristy setting, to appreciative locals. ⓐ Via Palermo 20 ⓘ 02 654 060 ⓛ Mon–Sat Ⓜ Metro: Lanza or Moscova

THE CITY

Osteria La Carbonella £££ ❾ Look for grilled meats and risotto with white truffles from nearby Alba. Bookings are a must.
ⓐ Via Terraggio 9 ⓣ 02 861 835 Ⓜ Metro: Cadorna

Cinemas & theatres

Piccolo Teatro/Teatro Strehler European theatre groups perform dramatic works at this Brera venue, in an exciting and interesting year-long festival schedule. ⓐ Largo Greppi ⓣ 02 7233 3222 ⓦ www.piccoloteatro.org (in Italian) ⓛ Oct–May Ⓜ Metro: Lanza

Teatro Smeraldo A venue for popular music and dance performances, Teatro Smeraldo hosts top international touring shows and solo acts. ⓐ Piazza Venticinque Aprile ⓣ 02 2900 6767 ⓦ www.smeraldo.it Ⓜ Metro: Garibaldi FS

Teatro Dal Verme Classical and semi-classical concerts are performed by touring groups and a variety of local music companies, from quartets to the symphony, in a small theatre near Castello Sforzesco. ⓐ Via San Giovanni sul Muro 2 ⓣ 02 2940 9724 ⓦ www.dalverme.org Ⓜ Metro: Cairoli

Bars, clubs & discos

Alcatraz Big-name groups, usually Italian and European (such as Exodus and Nuclear Assault), play during the week; at weekends it's DJs with dance music. ⓐ Via Valtellina 25 ⓣ 02 6901 6352 Ⓜ Bus: 90, 91, 92; Tram: 3

Blue Note This intimate jazz club opened a few years ago, and has kept a full house for live performances of name soloists and groups ever since. ⓐ Via Borsieri 37 (just south of Piazza Segrino)

CASTELLO SFORZESCO & NORTHWEST MILAN

☏ 02 6901 6888 ⓦ www.bluenotemilano.com ⏲ 21.00 and 23.30 Sat, 21.00 Sun Ⓜ Metro: Zara

Hollywood A dance club that has managed to stay *au courant* since the 80s, in the La Brera neighbourhood, despite the claustrophobic atmosphere, absurd coat-room policy and whopping entrance fee. Tuesday is R'n'B night. ⓐ Corso Como 15 ☏ 02 6598 996 ⓦ www.discotecahollywood.com ⏲ Tues–Sun Ⓜ Metro: Garibaldi FS

Roialto A stylish crowd of 30-somethings packs the bar after work for the Caribbean-style drinks and bounteous free buffet. ⓐ Via Piero della Francesca 55 (near Bullona FS station from Stazzione Nord) ☏ 02 3493 6616 ⏲ 18.00–02.00 Tues–Sat, 18.00–21.00 Sun

Room 97 British and other foreign students, and others under 25, hang out here, especially on Thursdays for R'n'B and 70s–80s tunes. ⓐ Corso Garibaldi 97/99 ☏ 02 653 810 ⓦ www.room97.it Ⓜ Metro: Moscova

Shocking Club The music is a good mix and the cocktail-hour buffet is generous, although you'll pay for it in the hefty entrance charge. Thursday draws university students; other nights you'll see a lot of models from the fashion houses listening to commercial, revival and house, or to international guest DJs. ⓐ Bastioni di Porta Nuova 10 ☏ 02 657 5073 ⓦ www.shockingclub.net ⏲ Tues, Thur–Sat Ⓜ Metro: Garibaldi FS

THE CITY

Southwest Milan

Don't let the number of churches in this part of Milan scare you. They contain some of the most interesting sights in the city, including a whopping trick played by the greatest of Milan's Renaissance architects, Bramante. Making up for all the art and culture south of the Duomo is the seriously swinging Navigli neighbourhood alongside the old canal. Closer to the Duomo, spend some time in the tangle of small streets between it and the University to experience a more characterful Milan – and to discover restaurants and cafés filled with locals.

SIGHTS & ATTRACTIONS

The sights in this quarter cluster in groups, several of them within a few streets of the Duomo, a couple to the west (only a short walk south from Santa Maria della Grazie) and two more almost on the way to the Darsena and the beginning of the Navigli. The old docks area, the Ticinese, is now a mix of boutiques, studios, trendy cafés and smart restaurants.

Navigli

Thank Leonardo da Vinci for one of the city's liveliest settings for after-hours fun, especially in good weather. He designed some of the canals that helped make Milan the economic power it still is, by giving it access to water transport. The barges are gone, but you can still ride on a boat through the canals to see part of the old maritime quarter. The 24-passenger *Viscontea* leaves the Darsena twice a day April through mid-September. Booking ahead is essential.
❶ 02 6702 0280 ⓦ www.navigamilano.it

Southwest Milan
0
250 metres
0
250 yards
N
Metro Stop
Cathedral
Information
Police Station
Airport
Railway Stn
Hospital
Acquario
Parco Sempione
Torre Branco
Palazzo dell'Arte
Castello Sforzesco
Stazione Ferrovie Nord
Palazzo Clerici
Museo Poldi Pezzoli
Casa d. Manzoni
Tort de'spus
Stadio Giuseppe Meazza (San Siro)
Cenacolo Vinciano
S. Maria delle Grazie
Palazzo Arese Litta
Civico Museo Archeologico
Duomo
Pinacoteca Ambrosiana
Palazzo Reale
Museo Nazionale della Scienza e della Tecnologia
S. Ambrogio
Università Cattolica
San Sebastiano
Santa Maria presso San Satiro
S. Lorenzo Maggiore
Parco Solari
Darsena
Stazione Porta Genova
Parco Ravizza
MONCUCCO
Buonarroti
Lanza
Cairoli
Cordusio
Pagano
Conciliazione
Cadorna
Wagner
S. Ambrogio
Duomo
Missori
S. Agostino
Porta Genova
Romolo
Famagosta
V. BELI
V. IPPOLITO NIEVO
VIA PALLAVICINO
V. MARIO PAGANO
VIA XX SETTEMBRE
V. LEGNANO
VIA GIOTTO
VIA L. ARIOSTO
C. VERCELLI
PIAZZA SANTA MARIA DELLE GRAZIE
C. MAGENTA
VIA DANTE
V. A. MANZONI
PIAZZA MERCANTI
PIAZZA DEL DUOMO
V. CARDUCCI
VIA SAN VITTORE
ELBA
PIAZZA PO
VIA G. BONI
VIA G. DEZZA
PIAZZA VESUVIO
VIALE PAPINIANO
V. EDMONDO DE AMICIS
V. TORINO
V. MAZZINI
V. VINCENZO FOPPA
VIA COLA DI RIENZO
VIA ANDREA SOLARI
VIA SANTA SOFIA
VIA QUADRONNO
VIA SAVONA
V. VIGEVANO
PIAZZA XXIV MAGGIO
V. G. GALEAZZO
VIA TORTONA
ALZAIA NAVIGLIO GRANDE
STRADA
RIPA DI PORTA TICINESE
V. F. ARGELATI
VIA GIAMBOLOGNA
PAVESE
SFORZA
C. S. GOTTARDO
V. CARLO TORRE
V. CASSALA
V. LIGURIA
V. TIBALDI
V. TOSCANA
NAVIGLIO
ASCANIO
VIA ETTORE PONTI
VIA ZUMBINI
ALZAIA
VIA CARDINALE
VIA GIUSEPPE MEDA
VIA BONGHI
VIA AICARDO
STRADA
VIALE FAMAGOSTA
V. GIOV.DA CERM.
VIA S. PAOLINO
V. L. MONTE
1
2
3
4
5
6
7
8
9
10
11
12

THE CITY

Piazza Mercanti

Hardly anything medieval in Milan is left, thanks to wars and zealous renewal projects, making this little enclave opposite the 16th-century law courts even more charming. On one side is the 1233 **Palazzo della Ragione**, political centre of medieval Milan, and the black-and-white marble Palazzo degli Osii, built in 1316, forms the other. The colonnaded open area was the market.

Just off Piazza del Duomo Metro: Duomo

San Lorenzo Maggiore

San Lorenzo is an example of early Christian basilica design, even though it has been changed over the centuries. The chapel of Sant'Aquilino, to the right near the entrance, still shows the original 4th-century mosaic decorations. In front of the basilica are Milan's best Roman remains, 2nd-century columns, part of a temple or a public bath that were moved here in the 4th century.

Corso Porta Ticinese 02 8940 4129 07.30–12.30, 14.30–18.30 Mon–Sat, 07.30–18.00 Sun; admission charge Metro: S. Ambrogio; Tram: 3, 20

San Sebastiano

Like a huge civic sigh of relief, this round church was built in thanksgiving by those who survived the plague in the late 1500s. It still has a bright joyful look, thanks to the enormous painting that fills the inside of the big central dome, and the glow of candles on the altars that surround the walls.

Via Torino 02 874 263 08.00–12.00, 15.00–17.00 Mon–Sat, 9.30–12.30, 15.30–19.00 Sun Metro: Duomo

---

The interior of San Sebastiano

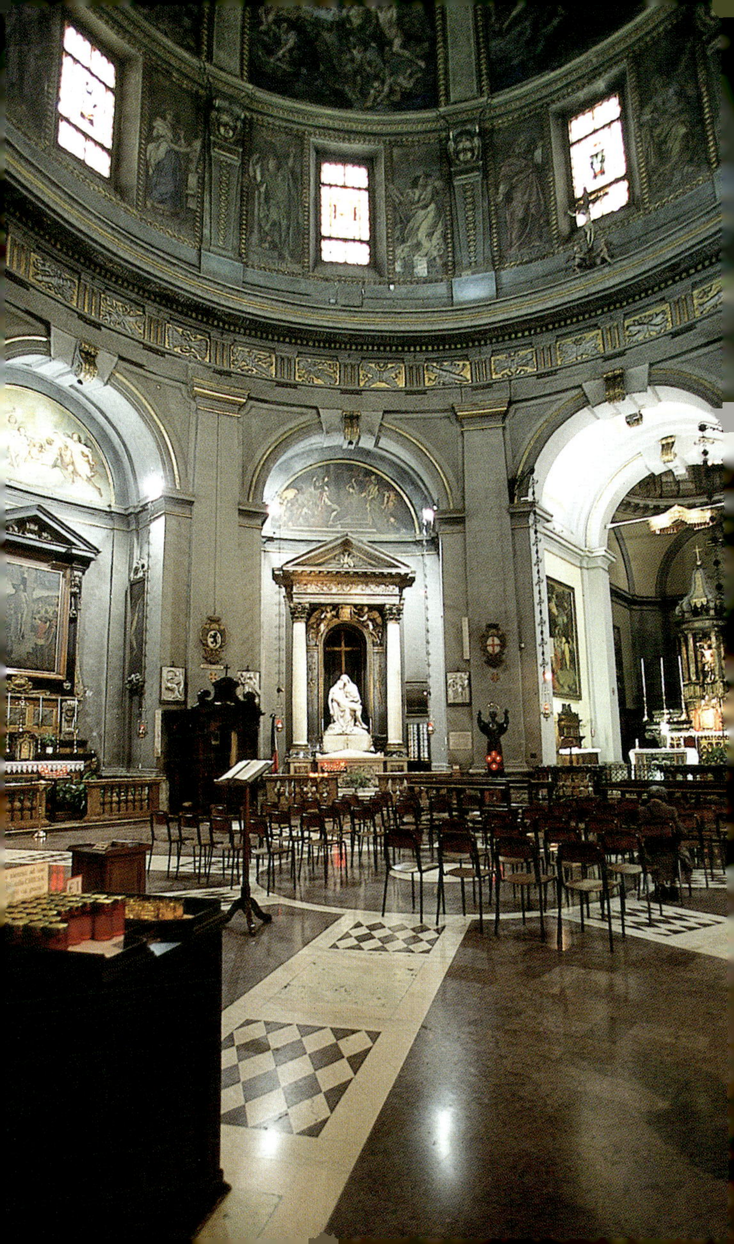

THE CITY

San Ambrogio
After the Duomo, this is Milan's most significant church. Highlights are the intricate carvings on the tops of the portico columns, the carved 4th-century Stilicone sarcophagus under the pulpit and the gold altarpiece by master goldsmiths in the time of Charlemagne. Through the last chapel on the right is the vivid mosaic dome of the original 4th-century Sacello de San Vittore.
ⓐ Piazza S. Ambrogio 15 ⓣ 02 8645 0895 ⓒ 07.00–12.00, 14.00–19.00 Mon–Sat, 07.00–13.15, 14.30–19.45 Sun; admission free, charge for Sacello de San Vittore Ⓜ Metro: S. Ambrogio

Sant'Eustorgio
In one of the repeated foreign raids on Milan, Sant'Eustorgio was sacked, and the relics of the Magi, which it had been built to house, were carted off. But this story takes an unexpected twist, because they were much later returned, and are still the centre of a festival on Epiphany (6 Jan). Balduccio's marble tomb of Stefano Visconti is an outstanding example of high Gothic, but the masterpiece that brings art lovers to the church is the Cappella Portinari, Milan's first real Renaissance room.
ⓐ Piazza S. Eustorgio ⓣ 02 5810 1583 ⓒ Church open 07.45–12.00, 15.30–18.30; Chapel open 10.00–18.00 Tues–Sun; 16.00–18.30 July–Aug; admission free to church, charge for chapel Ⓜ Tram: 3

Santa Maria presso San Satiro
It's hard to get any sense of the personalities of great historical figures and artists, but after seeing this church, it's easy to believe that Bramante had a sense of humour – as well as a brilliant talent for design. Step inside and your eye can't help but be drawn to the majestic deep vaulted sanctuary that stretches into an apse almost

SOUTHWEST MILAN

● *San Ambrogio*

as long as the main part of the church itself. Keep your eye on it as you walk forward, and watch it melt into an almost flat wall. Even when you know in advance that it's all a stucco illusion, it still looks so real that you doubt what you've read. Surely, Bramante must have chuckled to watch people as they discovered his trick.
ⓐ Via Torino 9 ⓣ 02 7202 1804 ⓒ 08.30–11.30, 15.30–17.30 Mon–Sat, 09.30–10.30, 16.30–17.30 Sun Ⓜ Metro: Duomo

THE CITY

Stadio Giuseppe Meazza (San Siro)
Football fans can see inside the stadium (even the locker rooms) on guided tours and brush up on the history of the sport at the Hall Of Fame for both of Milan's teams. With a ticket to the match, the museum is free until 30 minutes before kick-off.
ⓐ Via Piccolomini 5 ⓣ 02 404 2432 ⓦ www.sansirotour.com
ⓞ 10.00–17.00 (may vary on match days); admission charge
ⓜ Metro: Lotto; Tram: 24

CULTURE

The two museums in southwestern Milan offer, between them, something for everybody. One is filled with not just paintings by the great names in art, but drawings and, in the case of da Vinci, his plans for inventions. That theme is explored further in the lively science and technology museum, where da Vinci's plans have been brought to life with replicas and working models.

Museo Nazionale della Scienza e della Tecnologia Leonardo da Vinci (National Museum of Science and Technology)
You don't have to be a techie to love this museum, where the works of Leonardo da Vinci are shown in the light of their impact on later – even modern – technology. Da Vinci is Milan's favourite son and this museum shows off the inventor side of this quintessential Renaissance Man.
ⓐ V. S Vittore 21 ⓣ 02 4855 5200 ⓦ www.museoscienza.org
ⓞ 09.30–16.30 Tues–Fri, 09.30–18.30 Sat & Sun, Air transport section shorter hours; last admission 30 min before closing; admission charge ⓜ Metro: S. Ambrogio; Bus: 50, 54, 58, 94

SOUTHWEST MILAN

Pinacoteca Ambrosiana (Ambrosiana Art Mueum)

Based on the private collections of a cardinal, who built it in the early 1600s, the galleries are split between the priceless collection of early manuscripts and the paintings and drawings. Several small paintings by Brueghel are among the highlights.

ⓐ Piazza Pio XI 2 ⓣ 02 806 921 ⓛ 10.00–17.30 Tues–Sat; admission charge Ⓜ Metro: Duomo

RETAIL THERAPY

Stretching southwest from the Duomo, Via Torino is one of the city's main shopping streets, especially for shoes. Shops are aimed at a youngish set, and include all price ranges. At the far end of Via Torino is the Ticinese area, filled with artisans' studios and small speciality shops. From Largo Carrobbio, Corso di Porta Ticinese leads to the Navigli, another area with artisans' workshops.

Antiques and collectibles are the focus of the street market, the last Sunday of each month along the Naviglio Grande canal. Serious collectors go to the antique shops behind S. Ambrogio along Via Santa Marta and Via Lanzone. On Via San Giovanni you'll find smaller items, in shops that often specialise in one type of antique, such as glassware or scientific instruments.

Borgo Albina Beautifully detailed handbags and totes in original designs and all varieties of leather are made in the workshop.
ⓐ Alzaia Naviglio Pavese 6 ⓣ 02 8940 9326 Ⓜ Metro: Porta Genovese

Cavalli e Nastri Vintage clothing and accessories by the great designers. ⓐ Via Arena 1 ⓣ 02 8940 9452 Ⓜ Metro: S. Ambrogio

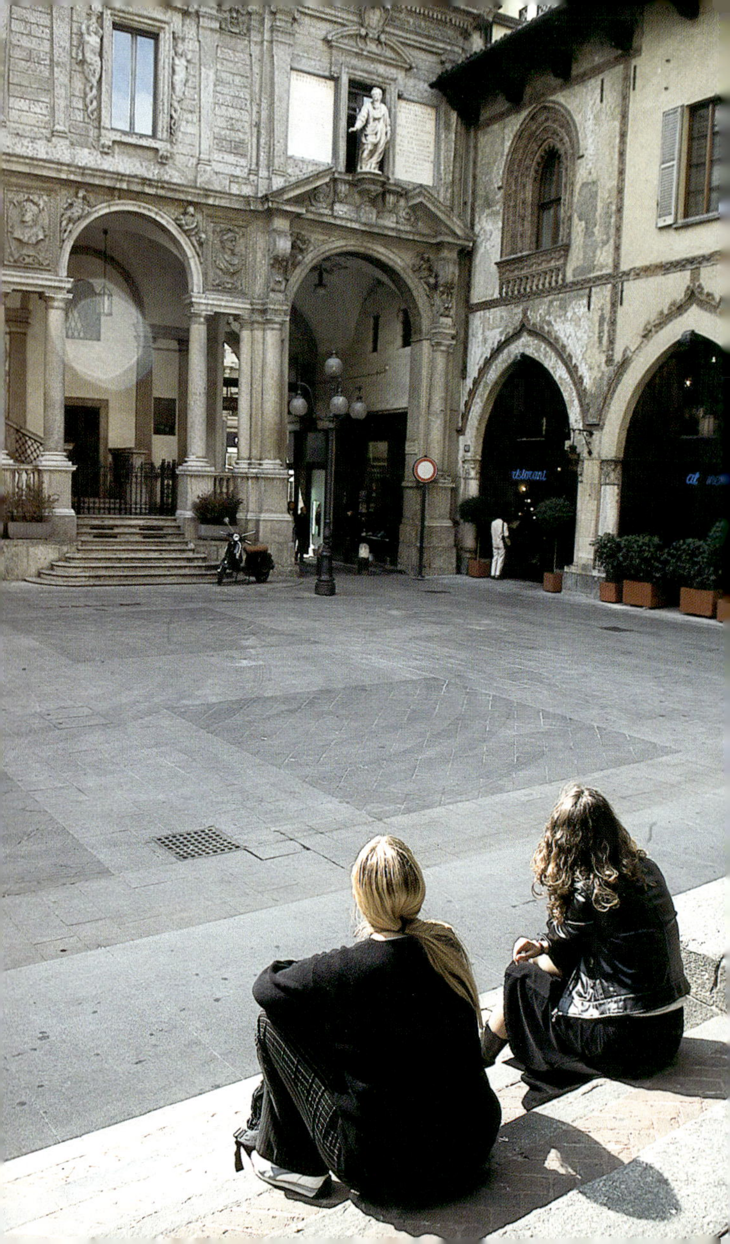

SOUTHWEST MILAN

Gandus La Velox Stop here for boxes and containers of all sorts, from cute gift boxes to unusual collectibles. ⓐ Via Asole 4 ⓣ 02 8635 2210 ⓜ Metro: Duomo

Lazzari Useful, well-designed fabric household goods, from laundry bags to dog beds. ⓐ Corso Porta Ticinese 70 ⓣ 02 422 4451 ⓜ Metro: S. Ambrogio

Papiniano Market The popular street market has everything from food and housewares to cut-price designer labels. ⓐ Viale Papiniano ⓣ 08.30–13.00 Tues, 08.30–17.00 Sat ⓜ Metro: Sant'Agostino; Tram: 20, 29, 30

TAKING A BREAK

The canal banks are lines with cafés and *pizzarie*, so there's no shortage of places to stop for a little bit of something. Some bars have food in the early evening, some have just a bowl of crisps.

La Briocheria di Rajmondo £ ❶ Ask for brioche (Milanese for croissant), filled (*sfoglitelle di ricotta*) or plain, or grab a slice of pizza for a pick-up. You'll have to eat it on the canal embankment, since there are no tables. ⓐ Via Scoglio di Quarto 3 ⓣ 338 406 5217 ⓛ until 02.00

20 (Vente) £ ❷ Trendy, arty (it's part bar, part gallery) and welcoming, 20 offers enough food to go with aperitifs that it might replace dinner altogether. Wednesday is student night, with drinks

◀ *Catching the sun in Piazza Mercanti*

THE CITY

and buffet for €5. ❷ Via Celestino IV 9 (at Via Gian Giacamo Mora) ❶ 02 837 6591 Ⓜ Metro: S. Ambrogio

Café Sarducci ££ ❸ An elegant, but amiable corner café near S. Ambrogio, with good bar snacks in the late afternoon. ❷ Via San Vittore 2 ❶ 02 890 0440 Ⓜ Metro: S. Ambrogio

Gattullo ££ ❹ A long-time favourite for really good panettone, plus other pastries, lunches and aperitifs. ❷ Piazza Porta Lodovica 2 ❶ 02 5831 0497 ⏰ 07.00–22.00 Tues–Sun Ⓜ Tram: 15

Pizzeria Tradizionale ££ ❺ The name pretty much sums it up, although they do serve a few fish dishes. ❷ Ripa di Porta Ticinese 7 ❶ 02 839 5133 Ⓜ Metro: Porta Genova

El Tropico Latino ££ ❻ With tables alongside the canal, this Mexican bar is a popular summer stop. ❷ Via Ascanio Sforza 41, at Via Lagrange ❶ 02 5810 4000

Shu £££ ❼ High-tech, high-style and high prices, but the drinks are good and there's food after work.
❷ Via Molino delle Armi 14 ❶ 02 5831 5720 Ⓜ Metro: Missori

AFTER DARK

The old canal area, the Navigli, is all about after dark (although you'll find its cafés open in the daytime, too). Music overflows into the streets, as do the throngs of 20- and 30-somethings that keep the area so lively.

SOUTHWEST MILAN

Restaurants

Although there are plenty of flashy high-end restaurants in these neighbourhoods, especially around Navigli, you'll also find cosy *trattorie* catering to the locals. Look for these as you sightsee during the day, in the streets between the Duomo and S. Ambrogio.

Govinda £ ❽ Vegetarian dishes, and no alcohol, are served in the restaurant operated by the Hari Krishna. ⓐ Via Valpetrosa 3 (just off Via Torino) ⓘ 02 862 417 ⓛ Tues–Sat ⓜ Metro: Duomo

Lanterna £ ❾ The neighbourhood trattoria serves satisfying hearty dishes with alpine influences. ⓐ Via Mercalli 14 ⓘ 02 5830 9604 ⓛ Mon–Sat ⓜ Metro: Missori

Mercanti ££ ❿ Warm, cosy interior, with tables on the medieval Piazza Mercanti in good weather. Local specialities are carefully prepared, even though this restaurant does get a good share of tourists because of its location just off Piazza del Duomo. ⓐ Piazza Mercanti ⓘ 02 805 2198 ⓛ Mon–Sat ⓜ Metro: Duomo

Osteria delle Vigne £–££ ⓫ Nice atmosphere, a good variety of tasty dishes and, as the name suggests, a very good wine list make this excellent value. Luncheon specials make it a bargain. ⓐ Ripa di Porta Ticinese 61 ⓘ 02 837 5617 ⓛ Mon–Sat, closed Aug ⓜ Metro: Porta Genova; Tram: 2

Trattoria Toscana ££ ⓬ The narrow entrance leads to an attractive dining room where Tuscan and northern dishes are well prepared. ⓐ Corso di Porta Ticinese 58 ⓘ 02 8940 6292 ⓜ Bus: 94; Tram: 3, 20

THE CITY

Bars, clubs & discos

Divina The décor is over the top and the house music is by well-known DJs, making this one of the best nightspots for dancing and mixing. ⓐ Via Molino delle Armi at Via della Chiusa ⓣ 02 5843 1823 ⓒ 23.00–04.00 Thur–Sun ⓝ Tram: 3, 15

Le Biciclette Modern art mixes with contemporary and experimental music aimed at the young-prof and arty set that come here for the stretched happy hour and stay for the show. ⓐ Via Torti at Conca del Naviglio ⓣ 02 5810 4325

Mama Café The daily 'happy wine' features local wines with light snacks. Weekend music is very eclectic: it might be jazz, rock 'n' roll, 1950s, even voices from the lyric opera. ⓐ Via Caminadella 7 ⓣ 02 8699 5682 ⓦ www.mamacafé.it ⓒ Closed Sun ⓝ Metro: S. Ambrogio

Puerto Alegre This pricey restaurant/bar offers entertainment and live music six nights a week. ⓐ Via Borsi 9 ⓣ 02 8942 0969 ⓒ Tues–Sun ⓝ Metro: Porta Genova

Scimmie Beside the canal in Navigli, with nightly live blues, rock and jazz, Scimmie is one of the city's best-known clubs. ⓐ Via Ascanio Svorza 49 ⓣ 02 8940 2874 ⓒ Mon–Sat ⓝ Metro: Porta Genova

Propaganda A Navigli district disco that adds occasional live shows, Propaganda attracts mainly students. ⓐ Via Castelbarco 11 ⓣ 02 5831 0682

◗ *A Roman bridge over a gorge, Lake Como*

OUT OF TOWN
trips

OUT OF TOWN

Lake Como

Romans fled sultry Mediolanum (Milan) in the summer for Lake Como's cooling breezes, and it's still not a bad idea. The Roman villas have been replaced by more modern ones, some built by royalty, some now owned by cinema stars and some you can stay in. Perhaps the prettiest of Italy's lakes, Como is shaped like the letter Y, deep and narrow and tightly enclosed between tall mountains. Views are simply spectacular from nearly anywhere – except the northern part of the lake, where the shore flattens out. Even in winter, the climate is mild and Como's shores are still green. In the spring and summer flowers bloom everywhere, especially in the Tremezzina Riviera, and many of the villa gardens are open to view.

The best way to explore lakeside villages is on foot, through narrow stone passages hung with vines. You can drive all the way round the lake (though the road between Como and Bellaggio is white knuckles all the way, so it's best to avoid it by using the cheap car ferry to cross). Como's southeast arm is less interesting, but you can bypass it with a car ferry from Varenna.

Frequent ferries visit most of the lakeside towns and a day's excursion gives time enough to look around several, since most attractions are within walking distance of the ferry landing. Economical day passes allow multiple stops. ❸ Navigazione Lago di Como, Piazza Cavour ❶ 031 579 211 Ⓦ www.navigazionelaghi.it

Trains run every 30 minutes to the town of Como, at the lake's southern tip, from Milan's Stazione Centrale, a ride of about 40 minutes. Shuttle trains from Milan's Stazione Nord arrive at Como's more centrally located Stazione Milano Nord, near the ferry dock, and are timed to meet the ferries. Como is close enough that travellers can stay here, touring Milan on day trips.

Lake Como
0 6 km
0 4 miles
N
SWITZERLAND
ITALY
Pizzo di Gino 2245
Monte Bregagno 2107
Gigna Settentrionale 2409
Lago di Mezzola
Gravedona
Cólico
S38
Abbazia di Piona
S340d
City
Large Town
Small Town
Motorway
Main Road
Minor Road
Airport
Railway
Porlezza
S340
Lago di Lugano
Menaggio
Lago di Como
Bellano
Varenna
T. Pioverna
Cadenabbia
Bellagio
Lenno
Tremezzo
Sala Comacina
Isola Comacina
Lago di Lecco
S36
S583
Brienno
Nesso
Magréglio
Mandello del Lario
S340
Canzo
Lecco
Cernobbio
Brunate
Como
Erba
S639
Lago di Pusiano
Lago di Annone
Lago Garlate
S583
A9
S342
Cantù
Milan Region
Italy
S36
S35

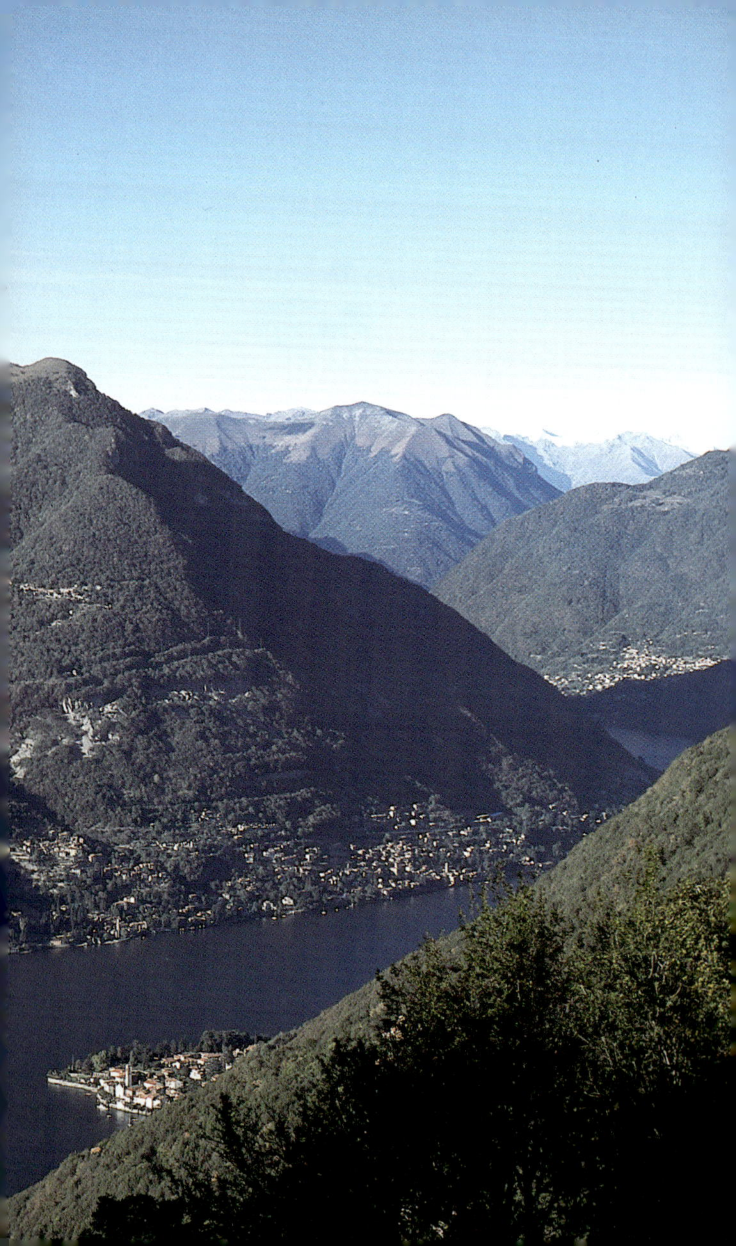

LAKE COMO

SIGHTS & ATTRACTIONS

Bellagio

Caught in the tip of the peninsula that divides the two southern arms of the lake, Bellagio has the most perfect setting on Lake Como and it makes the best of it with picturesque streets and elegant gardens. But the somewhat self-conscious prettiness doesn't diminish the appeal of its terraced and stair-stepped narrow streets, and icing-coloured buildings filled with boutiques and cafés. Passenger and car ferries connect to both shores.

The **Basilica di San Giacamo** is worth seeing for the detailed 12th-century stone carving behind the altar (ⓐ Piazza della Duomo ⓒ 08.00–12.00, 15.00–19.00). A lane behind the basilica leads to the gardens of **Villa Serbelloni**, covering the hillside with formal landscaping and exotic trees that frame views across Lake Como to the Alps (ⓣ 03 195 0204 ⓘ Tours 11.00 and 16.00 by reservation, Tues–Sun, mid-Apr–Oct, booked at the tourist information office in Bellagio; admission charge). Below, along the lake, are the gardens of **Villa Melzi d'Eril**, lovely for strolling. Azaleas and rhododendrons fill it with blooms in the spring and dark cypresses hide a serene Japanese garden (ⓐ Lungolario Marconi ⓣ 02 8699 8647 ⓒ 09.00–18.00 Apr–Oct; admission charge).

Brunate

Creaky vintage cars of Funiculare Brunate climb at a dizzying steep pitch for more than 1,000 m (3,300 ft) from Como's lakefront to spectacular views from café terraces in the village above. Or climb

◀ *View of Lake Como from Brunate*

OUT OF TOWN

the stone-paved path from the upper station to the tower at the top to see the Alps and the lakeshore towns to the north.
ⓐ Funiculare Brunate, Piazza de Gasperi ⓣ 031 303 608
ⓗ 06.00–22.30; admission charge

Cernobbio

On Como's western shore, Cernobbio's lakefront is dominated by villas set in gardens. The exiled English Queen Caroline stayed at the most glorious of them, Villa d'Este. Now an ultra-posh hotel, it is surrounded by elaborate Italian gardens open only to the villa's well-heeled guests. But Parco Villa Erba's gardens are open to the public on weekends.
ⓐ Via Regina 2 ⓣ 031 34 91 ⓗ 14.00–18.00 Sat, 10.00–18.00 Sun; admission free

Como

Trains from Milan arrive in Como, and although it's tempting to hop aboard a waiting boat to explore the lake, Como is worth a little time. The **Cortesella**, its old commercial streets that radiate from the shore, are still filled with interesting shops. At its centre is the **Duomo**, perhaps the best example anywhere of how 14th-century Gothic styles slipped into the Renaissance.
ⓐ Piazza del Duomo ⓣ 31 265 244 ⓗ 08.00–12.00, 15.00–19.00; admission free

At the centre of the leafy and walkable lakeshore promenade is Piazza Cavour, filled with cafés. Right on the shore, the temple-shaped building is **Tempio Voltiano**, a memorial/museum to native son Alessandro Volta (as in electric volt). In front of it is a moving

▶ *Sadly, the gardens at Villa d'Este are open only to guests*

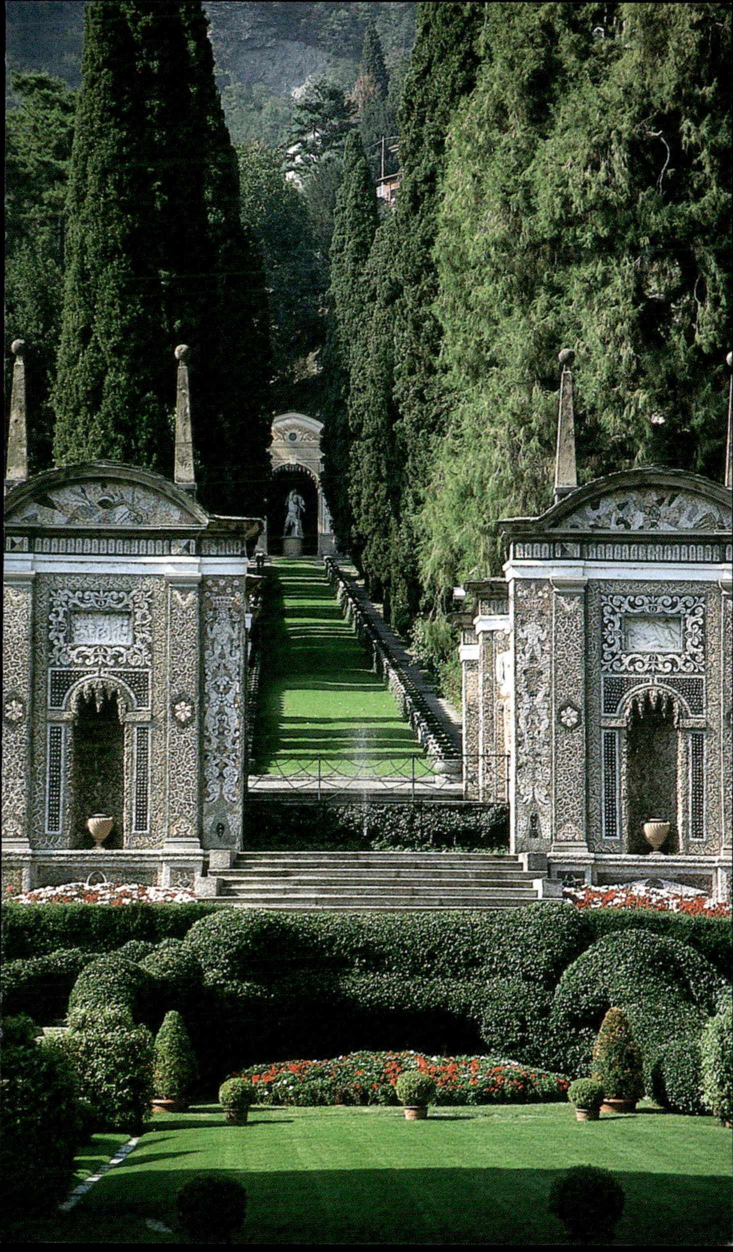

OUT OF TOWN

and sombre **Holocaust Memorial**, with quotes from victims in several languages, and a reminder of the many Italians among them. The promenade park continues to **Villa Olmo**, with its extensive and colourful gardens that are also a public park.

Isola Comacina

Mystery enshrouds the lake's only island, but through the mists of its often violent past flit a cast of characters straight out of history books: Atilla the Hun, Frederick Barbarossa, Lombard King Berringer, Queen Theodolinda, King Albert of Belgium and saints Abonde, Agrippa and Domenica. The latter three attest to its importance as a religious centre – barbarian hordes razed no fewer than five churches on the tiny island, at least one of them a Roman temple later consecrated by Christians. The ruins there today are the remains of the churches founded by the three saints, destroyed in the 1100s. These are connected by a single trail that loops around the island, leading uphill to the highest point, and to the foundations of **Sta Maria col Portico** before dropping to the remaining churches: walls and stone floors of the medieval **Basilica di Sant'Eufemia** below the later **Oratorio di Santi Giovanni**, Pietro e Paulo. Behind it, the **palaeo-Christian baptistery** has mosaics from the time of Charlemagne. Take a picnic lunch to this moody island and wander with ghosts from the Middle Ages; boats shuttle from Sala Comacina, where there is parking, or the lake boats stop here. 0338 459 9492 Operating 09.00–24.00 Mar–Oct, or Navigazione Lago di Como 031 579 211 www.navigazionelaghi.it

The Tremezzina Riviera

Even milder than the rest of the lake is this stretch of western shore, where it's not unusual to see outdoor cafés filled in February. The

LAKE COMO

steep hillsides behind Cadenabbia and Tremezzo are wrapped in year-round green, and lush plants native to southern climes thrive. Centrally located and with boat service to any part of the lake, the Tremezzina Riviera makes a good base for exploring by car or boat.
Villa Carlotta, the 18th-century palace of Prussian Princess Carlotta, has one of northern Italy's most famous gardens. Lined by camellias, rhododendrons, azaleas, palms and exotic trees, its paths open unexpectedly to show lake and mountain views, especially glorious in the early spring when everything is in full bloom.
ⓐ Via del Paradiso, Tremezzo ⓣ 0344 40 405 ⓦ www.villacarlotta.it
ⓒ 09.00–18.00 Apr–Sept; 09.00–11.00, 14.00–16.30 Mar & Oct; admission charge

On a point south of Tremezzo, **Villa Balbianello** sits in luxuriant perfectly groomed grounds. The baroque villa itself is not open to the public, but the gardens are. Late April through to mid-June is

> **WALKING AROUND COMO**
> Walking paths for all levels of energy are everywhere – short walking routes along the shore, high hikes along the mountainsides above. Some lead to sights missed by road-bound travellers, including huge boulders dropped by glaciers, castle ruins, waterfalls, Roman roads and Iron Age rock engravings. An excellent packet of cards, *By Foot in the Province of Como*, details walks in English and is available from provincial (APT) tourist offices. Several good walks begin in Bellagio, from a 20-minute amble to the tiny fishing village of **Pescallo**, the oldest settlement on that peninsula with waterside cafés and trattorie, to a strenuous hour rewarded by views of all three branches of the lake from the Belvedere at **Mulini del Perlo**.

OUT OF TOWN

the best time to visit, when azaleas and rhododendrons are in full bloom. Boats leave from nearby Lenno, or you can walk from the Lenno boat landing.

❶ 0344 561 10 ❷ 10.00–13.00, 14.00–18.00 Tues, Thur, Fri, 10.00–18.00 Sat & Sun, Apr–Oct; admission charge

Varenna

Car ferries shuttle across the lake into the little harbour where Varenna's pastel buildings cluster under cliffs, connected to the lake by a garden. The convent of **Villa Monastero**, abandoned since the 1500s, is planted in terraced formal gardens.

❶ 0341 295 450 ❷ www.villamonastero.it ❷ 09.00–12.00, 14.00–19.00 May–Sept, 09.00–12.00, 14.00–17.00 Oct–Apr

High above Varenna, 11th-century **Castello di Vezio** is open, with falconry demonstrations.

❶ Via Esino Lario ❶ 0335 465 186 ❷ www.castellodivezio.it
❷ 10.00–18.00 Apr–Oct; weekends only Nov–Mar; admission charge

To the north, in **Bellano**, the River Pioverna has cut a dramatic and eerie gorge through a solid rock mountain, its shape convoluted by caves and potholes. The trip through **Orrido di Bellano** is not for the acrophobic, on fenced walkways suspended over the chasm and the waterfall deep in its centre. It's especially spooky at night when the lights cast long dark shadows into its depths.

❶ 338 325 7117 ❷ 10.00–12.30, 14.00–23.00 Apr–Sept; 10.00–12.30, 14.00–17.00 Sat & Sun, Oct–Mar

LAKE COMO

CULTURE

Como's pleasures are more active and scenic than they are cultural, although some fine works of art hide in churches and the occasional villa is open to view. But two good museums in Como are worth a stop for those interested in their subjects: silk and early history.

Museo Civico

Two *palazzi* are chock-full of artefacts and exhibits, one giving a fascinating look at the early inhabitants of the lakes in Neolithic times, with tools and implements excavated nearby. Roman relics complete the picture of early Como, at the time of Julius Caesar.
ⓐ Via Vittorio Emanuele ⓣ 031 271 343 ⓑ 09.30–12.30, 14.00–17.00 Tues–Sat, 10.00-13.00 Sun; admission charge

Museo Didattico della Seta (Silk Museum)

Silk has been an important part of Como's economy since the 1500s, and the story of its manufacture fills this surprisingly interesting museum. Displays take visitors through the method of printing with the patterns that make Como silk distinctive.
ⓐ Via Valleggio 3 ⓣ 031 303 180 ⓦ www.museosetacomo.com
ⓑ 09.00–12.00, 15.00–18.00 Tues–Fri; admission charge Ⓝ Bus: 7

RETAIL THERAPY

The best thing to buy in Como is silk, the only question is where to buy it. Browse the shops in the old Cortesella to get an idea of what you like, then hit the markets. Silk goods to look for include women's scarves, dresses and blouses, lingerie and men's shirts and ties.

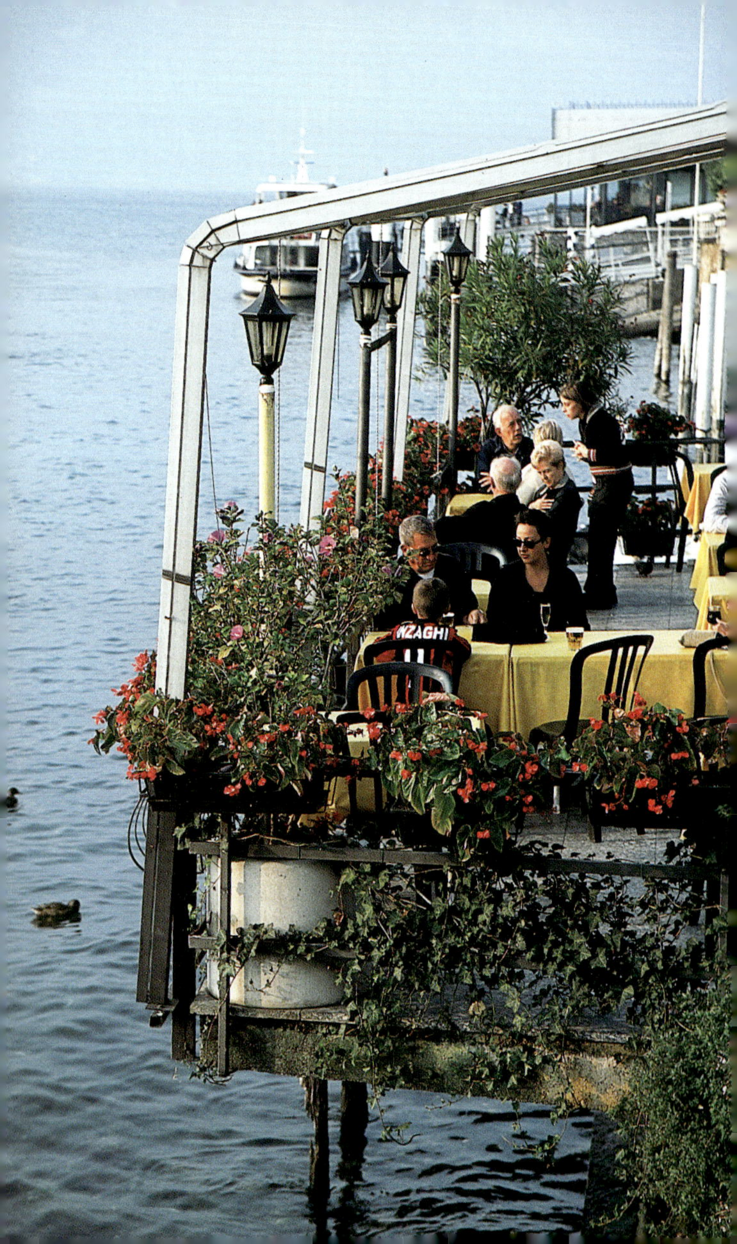

LAKE COMO

Binda Cut-price men's shirts, ties, women's scarves and more are in this silk manufacturer's factory store. ⓐ Viale Geno 6, Como ⓣ 031 386 1629

Frey Silk clothing, scarves and accessories are in the factory store of yet another Como firm, this one well located in the old town. ⓐ Via Garibaldi 10, Como ⓣ 031 267 012

Mantero Fine silks from the firm that supplies the big fashion names, including Nina Ricci. ⓐ Via San Abbondio 8, Como ⓣ 031 321 510

Martinetti Silk clothing is sold at a discount at the manufacturer's retail outlet. ⓐ Via Torriani 41, Como ⓣ 031 269 053 ⓛ 08.00–12.00, 14.30–18.00 Tues–Fri, 14.30–18.00 Mon, 08.00–12.00 Sat

On Tuesday and Thursday mornings and all day Saturday, the pavements along the old city walls become a street market, where you can find everything from clothing to hairbrushes. Be careful of pickpockets here. On Saturdays (except the first one each month) local craftspeople gather to sell in Piazza San Fedele, in central Como. The last Saturday of each month fills the streets and *piazze* with antiques vendors, creating gargantuan traffic snarls. Don't plan to drive to your hotel then.

    Bellagio has smart shops and boutiques, but remember that this is a resort town, accustomed to moneyed clientele on holiday, so while styles may be chic, prices will be the highest on the lake.

◀ *Enjoy a relaxed meal overlooking Lake Como*

OUT OF TOWN

TAKING A BREAK

The lake shore in every town will have a clutch of cafés lining the pavement and on terraces over the water. Along with coffee and stronger stuff to drink, most of these serve snacks and sandwiches. In Como, *gelati* and sandwiches are served aboard the *Lario*, an old motor-launch-turned-café, docked alongside the promenade.

Bistro del Ritorno £ Pizza, sandwiches, pasta and light dishes in a casual, friendly place with a terrace; a refreshing break from chi chi Bellagio. ⓐ Via E. Vitali 8 (off Via Roma from Piazza Mazzini), Bellagio ⓒ 031 951 915

Caffe' Nova Comum £ Cosy café for coffee or *gelato* during the day, until the stylish after-workers arrive for their aperitif. ⓐ Piazza Duomo 2, Como ⓒ 031 260 483

Il Sorbetto £ Check your email or plan your travels over coffee or *gelato* at this laid-back café/gelateria. ⓐ Salita Serbolloni, Bellagio

La Grotta £ Pizza, pasta and simple main dishes in a friendly atmosphere. ⓐ Salita Gernaia, Bellagio ⓒ 031 951 152 ⓒ Open daily June–Sept; Tues–Sun Oct–May

L'Altro Café £ Panini and piadini sandwiches and internet access in a relaxed and friendly setting where you're welcome to linger. ⓐ Via Diaz 28, Como ⓒ 031 260 664

Lostrano Bar £ Nice place to stop for a drink, with live music occasionally late in the evening. ⓐ Via Adamo del Pero 8, Como ⓣ 031 249 429

Novecento Cafè £ Aperitifs and a wide selection of teas, unusual in Italy. Foods include panini sandwiches and crêpes. ⓐ Viale Lecco 23, Como ⓣ 031 266 228

Pub Greenwich £ A casual central pub, where you can stop for a drink or light meal. ⓐ Piazza Giuseppe Terragni, Como ⓣ 031 267 872

Bar Argentino ££ The hip watering hole opposite the Duomo draws the after-work crowd with generous snacks to keep them ordering aperitifs. ⓐ Via Pretorio 1, Como ⓣ 031 304 455

Victoria Grill £–££ Good pizza, served in the grill room of the Hotel Victoria. ⓐ Piazza S Giorgio 5, Varenna ⓣ 0341 815 111

AFTER DARK

Nightlife around Lake Como is a far cry from that of swinging Lake Garda, but Como does offer a few good places to hear music, and its restaurants are good. Don't expect the glamour of Milan's nightspots, but don't expect the prices, either. And the fashion police don't guard the doors.

Restaurants
Albergo Ristorante Il Vapore £ A family inn, serving homey, hearty local dishes, including perfectly cooked lake fish. ⓐ Piazza T. Grossi 3, Mennago ⓣ 0344 322 29

OUT OF TOWN

Gatto Nero £ A meal with a view, both outstanding. Ask for a table with a view when booking. ⓐ Via Monte Santo 69, Cernobbio ⓣ 031 512 042

Osteria del Gallo £–££ Sample outstanding local wines by the glass at the bar or at a table, accompanied by a plate of individually prepared tapas – or something heartier and equally delicious, although it's not really a full-menu restaurant. ⓐ Via Vittani 16 ⓣ 031 272 591

Trattoria del Rana £–££ A casual, friendly trattoria where you'll meet more locals than tourists over generous plates of homestyle food. ⓐ Via Monte Vrappa 27, Tremezzo ⓣ 0344 40 602 ⓞ Wed–Mon, closed Oct

Il Solito Posto ££ Local favourites, including meaty osso bucco and hand made seasonal ravioli. ⓐ Via Lambertenghi 9, Como ⓣ 031 271 352

Ristorante Hosterietta ££ Risotto is the house speciality, available in a wide selection of combinations, including one with roasted red chicory. ⓐ Piazza Volta 57, Como ⓣ 031 241 516

Ristorante Silva ££ Fresh trout and other fish from the lake are the specialities at this legendary inn, a short way south of town beyond the Villa Melzi gardens. ⓐ Via Carcano 12, Localita Loppia, Bellagio ⓣ 031 950 322

LAKE COMO

Cinemas & theatres
Como has one theatre, Teatro Sociale (ⓐ Via Bellini ⓣ 031 270 170), although Villa Olmo hosts a number of concerts, performances and rehearsals. It's worth attending one just to see the interior, an impressive hall, three storeys tall with balconies. The four cinemas in Como show mostly Italian and lead international films.

Bars, clubs & discos
Il Birrificio di Como A cavernous microbrewery where you can see beer being made and sample the latest recipe. ⓐ Via Paoli 3, Como ⓣ 031 505 050 ⓦ www.ilbirrificio.it

Lido di Lenno On Friday and Saturday nights, this restaurant turns into a nightclub, but with no entrance charge and reasonably priced drinks. Dance on the covered dancefloor or on the beach. ⓐ Via Comoedia 1, Lenno ⓣ 0344 570 93 ⓦ www.lidodilenno.com ⓑ Bar open 16.00–04.00

Milonga Pub Live rock or jazz – and occasional others – almost every night, with good food, no dress code and reasonable prices. ⓐ Via Oltrecolle 23, Lipomo, Como ⓣ 031 28 00 52 ⓦ www.milongapub.it

Tartaruga Frequent live music shows and dancing until 03.00 in the morning. ⓐ Via Belvedere 12, Villa Guardia (about 20 km/12 miles from Como) ⓣ 031 483 290 ⓦ www.tartaruga.com

ACCOMMODATION

Hotel Engadina £–££ Modern and attractive rooms combine with a location close to the railway station and the lake. Free parking, air

OUT OF TOWN

conditioning, TV, bar, lift and a 24-hour desk make this good value.
ⓐ Vialle Roselli 22, Como ⓣ 031 570 008 ⓕ 031 576 487
ⓦ www.emmeti.it

Park Hotel £–££ An attractive modern hotel in the old section of the city, the Park has internet points, TV, a bar, parking and a lift. ⓐ Viale Rosselli 20, Como ⓣ 031 572 615 ⓕ 031 574 302
ⓦwww.emmeti.it

Terminus ££–£££ With all of the belle époque elegance of the Liberty style of architecture, this lakefront hotel in the heart of Como has recently added internet service, direct phones and even a sauna and gym (with massage available). ⓐ Lungo Lario Trieste, Como
ⓣ 031 329 111 ⓕ 031 302 550 ⓦ www.hotelterminus-como.it

Grand Hotel Tremezzo Palace £££ Built at the beginning of the 20th century, the hotel has retained its belle époque charm while adding mod cons. Facing onto the lake, its front rooms have magnificent views, while those on the back look out into the hotel's park-like terraced gardens. Breakfast (included) is among the most memorable anywhere. ⓐ Via Regina 8, Tremezzo ⓣ 034 440 446
ⓕ 034 440 201 ⓦ www.grandhoteltremezzo.com

Grand Hotel Villa Serbelloni £££ This former villa is the essence of genteel hospitality, with exceptional service, glorious décor and its own orchestra for dancing every evening. ⓐ Via Roma 1, Bellagio
ⓣ 031 950 216 ⓦ www.villaserbelloni.it

▶ *Relax in the hotel pool at Villa Serbelloni*

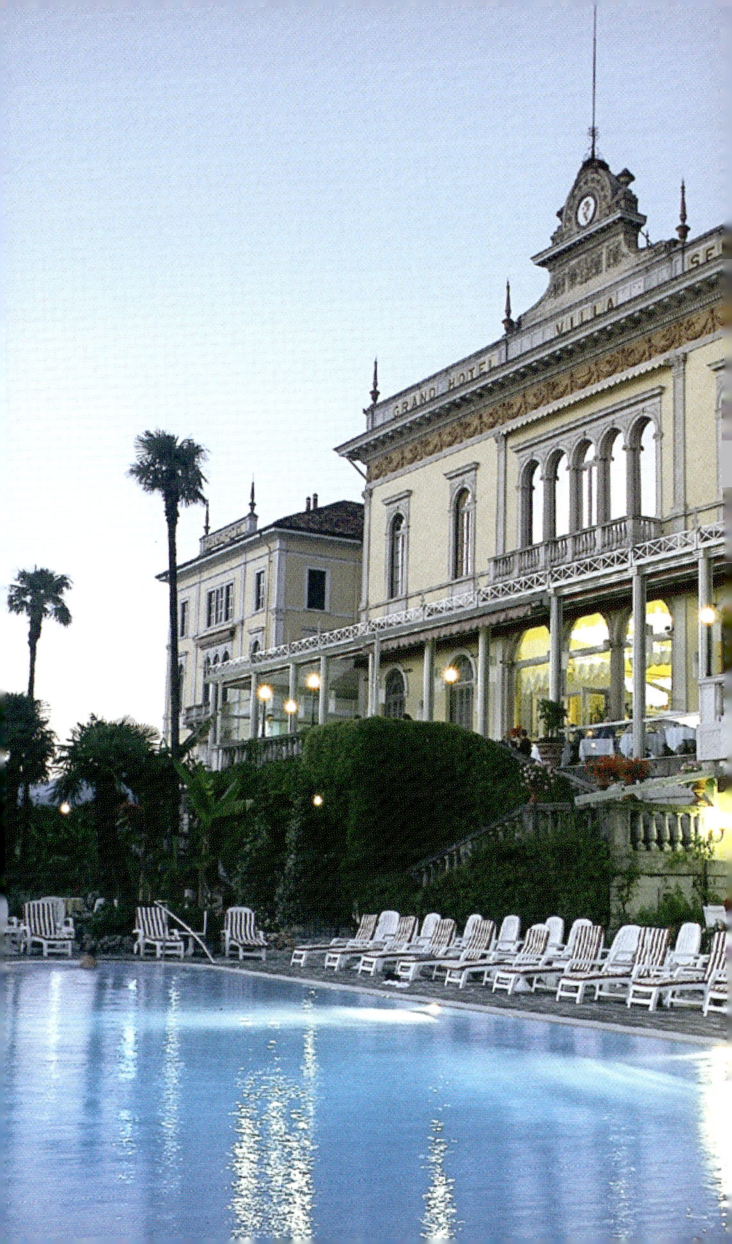
GRAND HOTEL
VILLA

OUT OF TOWN

Lake Maggiore

Although Italy can't claim all of this sprawling and scenic lake, it has all but the northern tip, which lies in Switzerland. Mountains surround it on all sides, sometimes rising almost straight from the shore, in other places sloping gently away. Either way, they give almost every lake view a good backdrop. For views down on the lake and into the layers of Alps that extend beyond it, you can take cable cars from the lakeside to several of the peaks.

A variety of boat transport – steamers, hydrofoils (*corse rapide*) and car ferries (*traghetti*) connect the shore towns, and roads circle the lake shore (➌ Navigazione Lago Maggiore ➊ 800 551 801 ⓦ www.navigazionelaghi.it). Towns on the southwest shore are connected to Milan's Stazione Centrale by train, while Laveno and points north on the eastern shore are on lines from Garibaldi and Cadorna stations.

Angera

The Borromeo family history is the history of the lake and of nearly all its towns, and you will bump into Borromeos at every turn. Meet them first in the imposing castle from which they guarded the southern entrance to the lake. The original medieval defensive structure of **Rocca Borromeo** (Borromeo Castle) is still intact. Interesting only to serious doll collectors are the **Museo della Bambola** displays of 1,000-plus dolls. ➌ Via alla Rocca ➊ 0331 931 300 ⓦ www.roccaborromeo.it ⓛ 09.00–18.00 Apr–Sept, 09.00–17.30 Oct; admission charge

Even the grumpiest museum-hater will smile – maybe even laugh out loud – in the wonderfully quirky **Museo dei Transporti** in neighbouring Ranco. You can climb onto vintage tram cars, peer

Lake Maggiore
0
10 km
0
6 miles
City
Large Town
Small Town
Motorway
Main Road
Minor Road
Airport
Railway
N
Locarno
Ascona
S34
Lago Maggiore
Brissago
SWITZERLAND
A2
ITALY
Cannobio
Monte Zeda
2156
Cannero Riviera
Breno
Luino
Lugano
S34
Premeno
Bee
Ghiffa
Caldé
ondotoce
Verbania
Intra
Pallanza
S233
Baveno
Laveno
Isole Borromeo
Stresa
Cuvio
Alpino
Sta Caterina
Monte Campo dei Fiori
1226
Bisuschio
S33
Besozzo
Belgirate
Lago Maggiore
Varese
Lago Varese
Ranco
Angera
Azzate
A8
Arona
Milan Region
Italy
Sesto Calende
A8-A26
S33
Gallarate
A26
Bogogno
S32
Malpensa
Cardano al Campo
A8

OUT OF TOWN

through the windows of Pope Pius IX's railcar chapel, ride the escalator into a subway station, follow the coal-cart into a coal mine and admire carriages and conveyances of the formerly famous. You need to look up, down and all around, and to follow every little passageway so as not to miss something. ⓐ Off S629, Ranco ⓛ 10.00–12.00, 14.00–18.00 Tues–Sun; admission free

Arona

A good base if you arrive from Milan by train, Arona has plenty of hotels and restaurants, plus good access to transport around the lake. Stop at the Turismo for boat schedules, maps and advice (ⓐ Pzle Duca d'Aosta ⓣ 0322 243 601). While in town, take advantage of what may be your only opportunity to see the world through the eyes of a saint. On a hillside just north of town stands the 23.5 m (75 ft) tall statue of **San Carlo Borromeo**. Climb the 145 stairs to the head, from which you can view the world through one eye. ⓐ Off S33, north of town ⓛ 09.15–12.30, 14.00–18.30 Apr–Sept; Sat & Sun only Oct & Mar

Isole Borromeo (Borromean Islands)

The undeniable highlight of the lake is this group of islands in Golfo Borromeo, near Stresa. You can see them all in one day or make separate trips; you can even stay overnight on the smallest (and most charming) of them. It's hard to see them all by using the regular lake steamer, whose schedules don't give you enough time or can leave you there too long. For the most flexibility, spend a little more for a day ticket from one of the taxi services that allow you to move at will among the islands. The *bigliateria* (kiosk) next to Stresa's steamer landing has tickets and details.

◗ *Statue of San Carlo Borromeo, Arona*

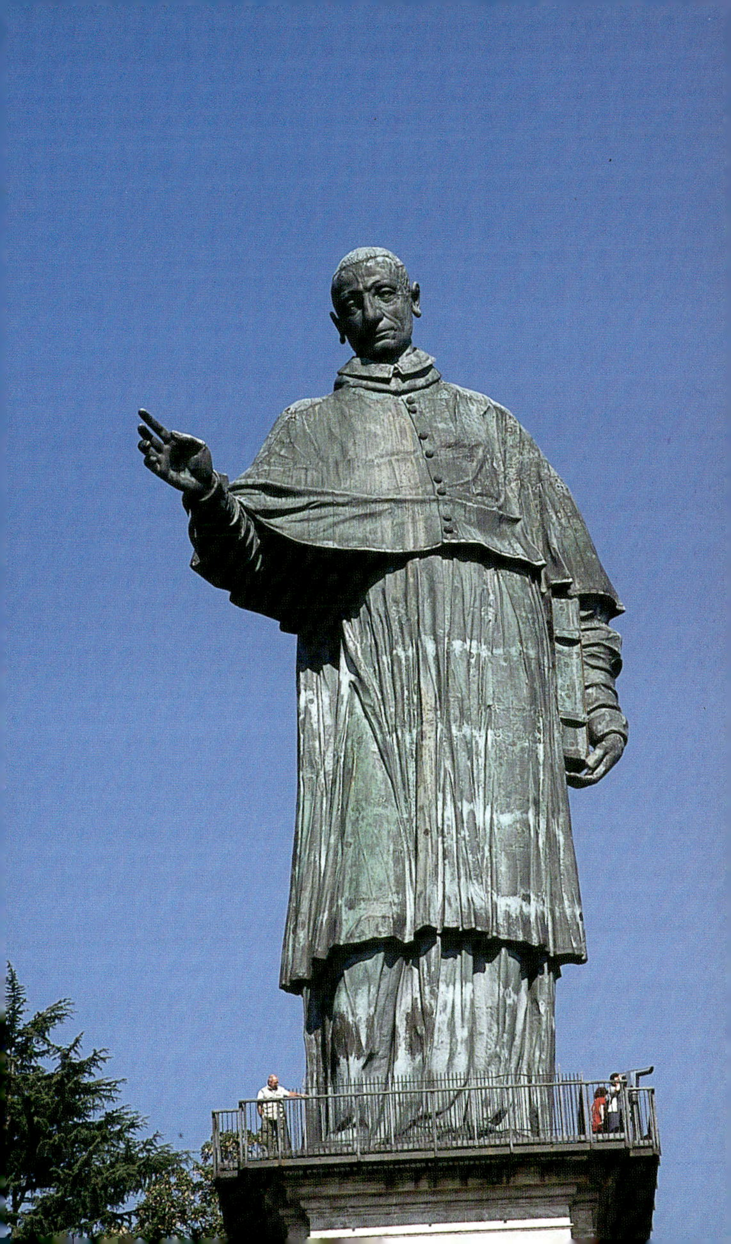

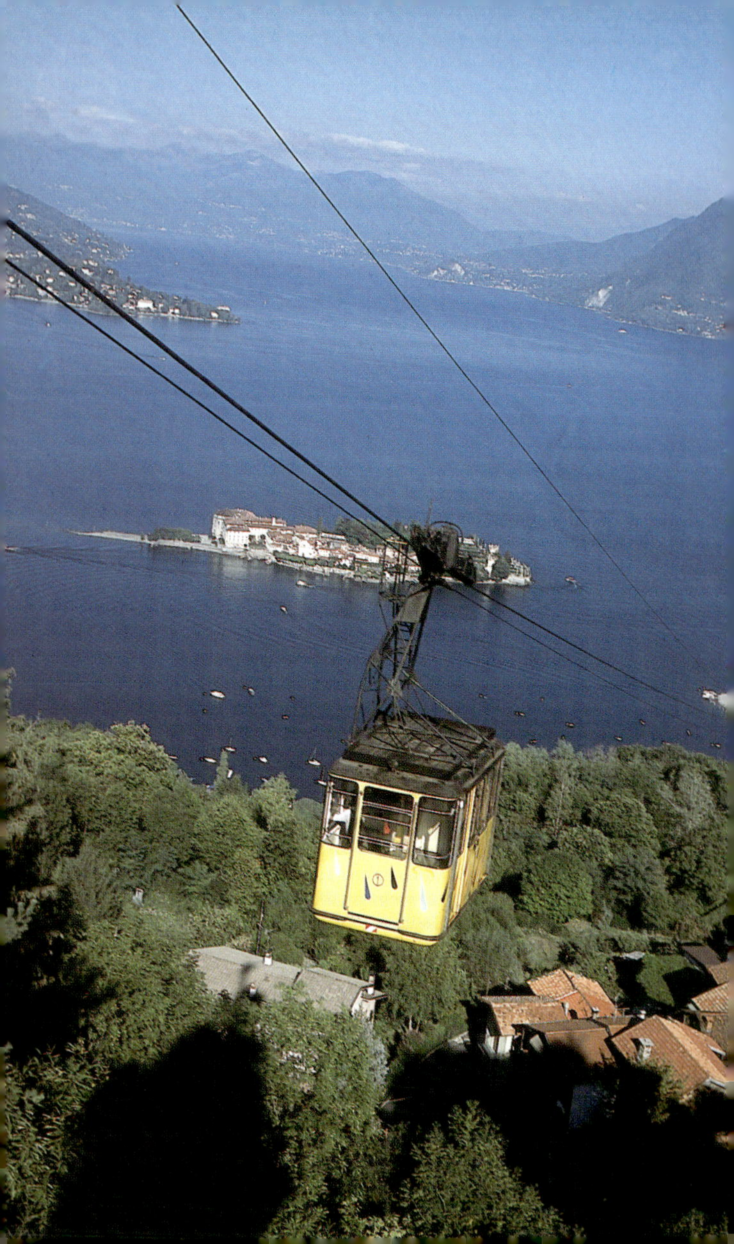

LAKE MAGGIORE

Isola Bella

Begin with this island. Everything here is over-the-top, from the astonishing giant Mannerist figures in the gold-and-stucco Throne Room of **Palazzo Borromeo** to the improbably fussy terraced gardens (❶ 0323 305 56 ❿ www.borromeoturismo.it ❶ 09.00–17.30 Apr–Sept, 09.00–17.00 Oct; admission charge). From the faux grotto on the ground floor, step out the back door into the gardens. Climb to the top for smashing views of the palace, the lake and the patterned flowerbeds below; it's not so overwhelming from up there and the flowerbeds are designed for aerial viewing. A tangle of narrow passageways leads back to the boat landing, lined by a mix of chi chi boutiques and kitsch souvenir stalls. Along the shore are cafés and restaurants.

Isola Madre

After the regimented and ornamented fussiness of Isola Bella, let your spirit run free in the spacious and serene garden park covering most of Isola Madre. Paths lined by exotic trees wander circuitously past lawns highlighted by flowerbeds, and continue around the shore. The southern shore is a terraced promenade. The villa there is smaller and less opulent, worth touring to see the wonderful marionette theatre collections on the top floor. ❶ 0323 312 61 ❿ www.borromeoturismo.it ❶ 09.00–15.30 Apr–Sept; 09.00–17.00 Oct; admission charge

Isola Pescatore

The tiniest of the islands has no palaces and no gardens; there hardly seems to be room enough for the cluster of candy-coloured

◐ *The cable car in Monte Mottarone overlooks Isola Bella*

houses and the narrow streets. Fishing boats are tied along the shore, and you may see someone mending nets. Ernest Hemingway, who wrote *A Farewell to Arms* in a nearby mainland hotel, liked this little island and its fishermen. The cafés he frequented are still here.

LAVENO

A car ferry shortens driving distances around the lake by shuttling cars across to the Intra wharf in Verbania (ⓐ Navigazione Lago Maggiore ⓣ 800 551 801 (free call) ⓦ www.navigazionelaghi.it). An odd little bucket-like gondola carries passengers to the top of **Sasso del Ferro** for views of the lakes and mountains. One of the lake's prettiest spots is south of Laveno, the 13th-century hermitage **L'Eremo di Santa Caterina del Sasso Ballaro**, built into the face of a cliff between the villages of Cerro and Reno. Take the steep stone steps down the banking to see it, or photograph it from the lake steamer as it passes close (ⓛ 08.30–12.00, 14.30–18.00 Apr–Oct; 09.00–12.00, 14.00–18.00 Sat & Sun, Nov–Feb; admission free). To the north of Laveno, the picture-perfect little harbour of **Calde** hides behind a rock promontory. Follow signs to the popular restaurant, La Vela, to find it from the main lake road.

From Laveno, it's an easy 12 km (7 miles) drive to pretty little **Lake Varese**, with its reedy lake shore, birdlife and nature reserve. The old town of Azzate makes a good stop, with several cafés and fine dining in a medieval manor house.

On the way is **Villa della Porta Besozzo**, a grand villa, set in a splendid baroque garden. ⓐ Casalzuigno ⓣ 0332 624 136 ⓛ Villa 10.00–13.00, 14.00–17.00, park 10.00–17.00 Tues–Sun, Oct–Nov; 10.00–13.00, 14.00–18.00, park 10.00–18.00 Tues–Sun, Feb–Sept; admission charge

STRESA

Old money built Stresa, in the days when wealthy Milanese escaped the heat by bringing their families to its grand lakefront hotels for the summer. Evidently there's enough new money to keep the sumptuous digs thriving, because they fairly sparkle with fresh paint and polish. The moneyed mood is kept up in the boutiques that line its well-kept streets.

Boats leave from its waterfront for Isole Borromeo, and from Piazalle Lido, north of the centre of town, a cable car to the top of **Monte Mottarone** provides beautiful views down at the hotels and the islands. From the top you can see Lakes Maggiore and Orta (a smaller lake to the west), and the Alps. If it's clear, you can see Milan (a Funivia il Mottorone t 0323 303 99 w www.terradeilaghi.com 09.30–18.00; admission charge). Stop halfway for a short walk to **Giardini Alpina** (Alpine Gardens), where 800 varieties of alpine plants from mountains all over the world cover a hilltop. Views from the gardens are good, too, and your cable car ticket includes admission. t 0323 201 63 09.00–18.00 Tues–Sun, Apr–mid-Oct

Villa Pallavicino is on the shore south of Stresa, sitting in a 20-ha (50-acre) park filled with more than 40 species of exotic animals and birds – kangaroos, zebras, llamas, flamingoes – and formal gardens in beds of solid colour. Children will like the petting section with baby animals. a Rte S33 t 0323 315 33 w www.parcozoopallavicino.it 09.00–18.00 Mar–Oct; admission charge

VERBANIA

The former towns of Pallanza, Intra, Suna, Fondotoce, Trobaso and Possaccio make up Verbania, which sometimes makes it confusing for strangers who look for these places on a map. **Madonna di**

OUT OF TOWN

Campagna, on the road between the Intra and Pallanza settlements, is a beautiful Romanesque church whose building spans from the 12th century to the 16th. At Fonda Toce is the **Reserva Naturale di Fondo Toce**, a reed-filled bird habitat at the delta of the River Toce. Footpaths and bike trails wander through the wetlands, and tent pitches are inside the reserve. Book for guided walks and motorboat cruises with park naturalists at the office (@ Via Canale 48, Verbania (Fondatoce) ❶ 0322 240 239 ❷ 09.00–12.00, 14.00–17.00 Mon–Fri, 09.00–12.00 Sat). The gardens of **Villa Táranto** combine the formal terraces, pools and rose gardens of Italian gardens with the flowing lines of an English garden park filled with thousands of exotic and native trees. The lake's mild climate allows more than 20,000 plant varieties to grow here. @ Pallanza ❶ 0323 556 667 ❷ 08.30–18.30 Apr–Oct; admission charge

SWISS MAGGIORE

Only three boats a day run from the southern part of the lake to Locarno, in Switzerland, but several more leave from Luino. Or, at 09.30 a hydrofoil from Arona arrives in Locarno before lunch, a good scenic day trip. The easiest way to see the other towns in Swiss Maggiore is by bus No 21 from Locarno, or to drive across the border. The crossing is usually fast. In either case, you will need your passport, since Switzerland is not a member of the EU.

ASCONA

Ascona looks like a Swiss version of Italy – a little too neat and orderly. The signs and the food are Italian, but you know someone else has a hand in arranging things. It's not a bad combination, though browsing in boutiques and galleries and strolling the **Lungolago** promenade are about all there is to do here.

LAKE MAGGIORE

BRISSAGO

The town barely has room to perch in the narrow space between mountain and lake, but has made room for a kilometre-long (½-mile) promenade, the **Lungolago**. More warm-climate plants grow outdoors on the nearby island, **Isola Brissago**, which lake waters keep above freezing temperatures all winter. The botanical garden houses medicinal plants, some extinct in the wild. ❶ 091 791 4361 ⓦ www.isolebrissago ⏰ 09.00–17.00 Apr–Oct; admission charge. Go by boat from Porto Ronco, 2 km (1 mile) north of Brissago.

LOCARNO

The odd curving shape of Locarno's central **Piazza Grande** follows the original shoreline, before receding waters moved it away and the space was paved with river stones to form the *piazza*. Behind are twisted narrow streets, arcades and garden-filled courtyards with medieval houses and fountains. Near the railway station, a funicular takes passengers to **Orselina** for views and access to a *funivia* (cable car) bound for higher **Cardada**. Locarno is the starting point for the scenic Centovalli train excursion, on vintage railway carriages.

RETAIL THERAPY

For swish little boutiques, head straight for Stresa, whose streets are lined with them. For slightly less expensive shops, try the settlement of Intra, in Verbania, where the car ferry from Laveno lands. Laveno is known for its ceramics, and several shops sell examples of it. A museum in a *palazzo* in the adjoining village of Cerro is devoted to it. ⓐ Frazione Cerro ❶ 0332 666 530 ⏰ 14.30–17.30 Tues–Thur, 10.00–12.00, 14.30–17.30 Fri–Sun, Sept–June; 14.30–17.30 Fri–Sun, July–Aug; admission charge

OUT OF TOWN

Several towns have weekly markets, the largest of which is on Wednesday in Luino. Smaller, but with somewhat better merchandise, is the Saturday street market in Intra. A sharp eye will turn up bargains and the occasional local craftsperson or farmer with speciality foods, such as jars of wild berry preserves. On S34 in Fondotoce (Verbania) are several factory outlets of major Italian brands.

Alberti Libraio The bookshop concentrates on local culture, maps, guides and history of the lake and its surrounding towns. Look here for hiking maps and guides. 🅐 Corso Garibaldi 74, Verbania (beside the Cathedral in Intra) 🅣 032 340 2534 🅦 www.albertilibraio.it

TAKING A BREAK

Finding cafés, pizza shops and snack bars is easy in any of the lake towns. Just head for the water and you're sure to find at least one occupying a terrace or perched on the shore.

🔺 *The entertaining transport Museum at Ranco*

Monti's Café £ Wine bars – especially ones as laid-back and friendly as this one – are not as common in small lake towns as in the city. ⓐ Via A. Volta 47, Azzate (Lake Varese) ⓣ 0332 458 583

AFTER DARK

Nightlife is not a strong suite around Lake Maggiore, and is more likely to involve a leisurely dinner on a romantic lakeside terrace than dancing until 04.00. Most people come to Maggiore to get away from the city, instead of bringing it with them. But if you're feeling withdrawal symptoms, ask around and you might find a local spot with a DJ on Saturday night.

Restaurants

Boccon di Vino £–££ A little *osteria* with a blackboard menu, but a chef who knows his stuff. Whatever the day's pasta combo is, order it. ⓐ Via Troubetzkoy 86, Verbania ⓣ 0323 504 039

La Bruma del Lago £–££ Pasta variations go beyond the ordinary offerings, in this brightly decorated little restaurant in a cute post-modern setting. ⓐ Corso Mazzini 6, Belgirate

Taverna del Pappagallo £–££ The pizza and focaccia are baked in the wood-fired oven of this attractive family-run restaurant, close to the boat landing, behind the church. ⓐ Via Principessa Margherita 46, Stresa ⓣ 0323 304 11 ⓦ www.tavernapappagallo.com

Monnalisa ££ Dine in sight of the lake on well-prepared traditional Italian dishes, with attentive staff and attractive décor. ⓐ Via Poli 18, Arona ⓣ 03 2246 332

OUT OF TOWN

Osteria Degli Amici ££ Traditional Italian and Piedmontese fare is well prepared, and served in three pleasant dining rooms and a vine-covered terrace, for al fresco dining. ⓐ Via Anna Maria Bolongaro, Stresa ⓣ 03 2330 453

Piccolo Lago ££ Inspired combinations such as ravioli filled with artichoke and prawns make this modest restaurant popular. ⓐ Via Filippo Turati 87, Fondotoce (Verbania) ⓣ 0323 586 792

Ristorante Belvedere ££ Nicely prepared fish and handmade pastas are served in a romantic vine-hung terrace overlooking the lake. ⓐ Via Piave 11, Ranco ⓣ 0331 976 609

Ristorante Pescatori ££ At the lakefront you'll find this popular local restaurant, which specialises in the seafood of the lake, and beyond. Of course they also have pasta and traditional mains.
ⓐ Lungo Lago Marconi 27, Arona ⓣ 03 2248 312
ⓦ www.ristorantepescatori.it

Ristorante Piemontese ££–£££ In downtown Stresa, the Piemontese has a fine collection of local speciality dishes. Dine in their elegant dining room or on the pergola terrace. ⓐ Via Mazzini 25, Stresa
ⓣ 03 2330 235

Ristorante Verbano ££–£££ Eat on a terrace with a view of Isola Bella and the local boat traffic, while savouring lake fish and traditional dishes. ⓐ Isola Pescatore, to the right from the boat dock

Locanda dei Mai Intees £££ The chef-owned restaurant is set in a medieval manor house with priceless frescoes, but they pale in comparison to the delicate pastas and mains featuring locally grown ingredients. Well worth splurging. ◉ Via Nobile Claudio Riva 2, Azzate (Varese) ◉ 03 3245 7223 ◉ www.mai-intees.com

Il Sole di Ranco £££ One of northern Italy's finest restaurants, with two Michelin stars to prove it. Presentations and service are as outstanding as the creative dishes. It's well worth a splurge. ◉ Piazza Venezia 5, Ranco (Angera) ◉ 03 3197 6507 ◉ www.ilsolediranco.it

Cinemas, music & theatres

All the larger lake towns have at least one cinema, although films will nearly always be in Italian. Several also have occasional free lakeside concerts and music events; local tourist offices will have schedules of these.

A major international event for film fans is the **Festival del Film di Locarno**, when the main square, Piazza Grande, in Locarno (on the Swiss end of Lake Maggiore) becomes a giant outdoor cinema each evening. This mid-August event draws crowds from all over Europe, so be sure to book lodgings early.

Now more than 40 years old, **Settimane Musicali di Stresa e del Lago Maggiore** (Stresa-Lake Maggiore Music Weeks) begin in late July and last through mid-September. Most of the two dozen performances are scheduled for late August through mid-September, and they take place at Stresa, on the two larger Borromean Islands and in other lakeside towns. For a complete schedule, contact Settimane Musicali di Stresa e del Lago Maggiore ◉ Via Carducci 38, 28838 Stresa ◉ 0323 310 95 or 0323 304 59 ◉ 0323 330 06 (as for English language operators) ◉ www.stresa.net/settimanemusicali

OUT OF TOWN

ACCOMMODATION

Albergo Sempione £ The Albergo Sempione is on the lakefront promenade near the pier for the Borromeo Islands. Simple but attractive, it is a good buy as 12 of its 17 rooms have views of the lake. ⓐ Corso Italia 46, Stresa ⓣ 03 2330 463 ⓕ 03 2330 463 ⓦ www.albergosempione.it

Hotel Le Palme £ This attractive modern hotel with balconies has parking, a garden, tennis courts and even a solarium with views of the lake. The rooms have the expected mod cons. ⓐ Corso Cavour 130, Dormelletto (Arona) ⓣ 03 2249 7971 ⓕ 03 2249 7975

Locanda La Capuccina £ Agroturismo lodging is in a nicely renovated 16th-century farmhouse, a short distance west from Arona on the S142. Attractive rooms and a fine restaurant serving farm-raised produce, cheese and a wine cellar. ⓐ Via Novarra 19/B, La Capuccina, Cureggio ⓣ 03 2283 9930 ⓕ 03 2288 3691 ⓦ www.emmeti.it

Piccolo Lago £–££ Better known for its excellent restaurant, this little *locanda* also has 12 rooms with balconies overlooking the lake. You have to cross the road to get to its lakeside pool. ⓐ Via Filippo Turati 87, Fondotoce ⓣ 0323 586 792

Best Western Hotel Milano ££ Lake-lovers will like this small hotel (only 47 rooms) sitting right on the lake with a private beach. The bright terrace dining room overlooks the water.

◗ *Stay in style and luxury at Grand Hotel des Iles Borromees*

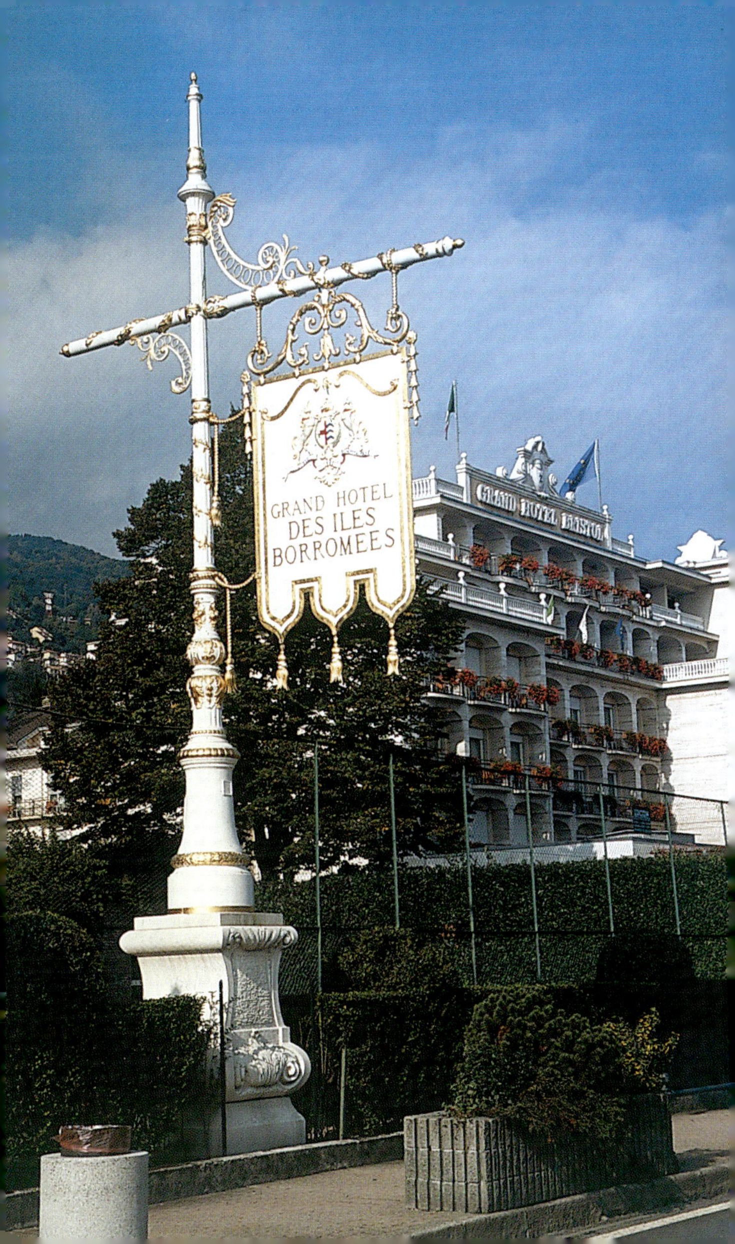
GRAND HOTEL
DES ILES
BORROMEES
GRAND HOTEL BRISTOL

OUT OF TOWN

Via Sempione 4, Belgirate-Novara ❶ 03 2276 525 ❷ 03 2276 295
❸ www.bestwestern.it

Best Western Villa Carlotta ££ Situated right on the lake, this large old but well-restored hotel has its own gardens for walking and attractive rooms with internet points. ❶ Via Sempione 121/125, Belgirate ❷ 03 2276 461 ❸ 03 2276 705 ❹ www.bestwestern.it

Grand Hotel des Iles Borromees £££ Built in 1861 and renovated in 1991, this is the Grand Dame of the lake. Simply elegant and luxurious. ❶ Lungolago Umberto, Stresa ❷ 03 2393 8938 ❸ 03 2332 405 ❹ www.borromees.it

Il Sole di Ranco £££ The windows of the guest rooms in this elegantly furnished villa overlook its gardens and the lake. The only thing better than staying in this warm family-run hotel is eating in the superb Michelin-rated restaurant. ❶ Piazza Venezia 5, Ranco ❷ 03 3197 6507 ❸ 03 3197 6620 ❹ www.ilsolediranco.it

Locanda dei Mai Intees £££ This small hotel is a medieval adventure in luxury. Furnishings are Renaissance but the baths are luxurious 21st century and dining in the outstanding restaurant is in full view of recently discovered 15th-century frescoes. ❶ Via Nobile Claudio Riva 2, Azzate (on Lake Varese) ❷ 03 3245 7223 ❸ 03 3245 9339 ❹ www.venere.com

◗ *Watching the sunset over Lake Como from Bellagio*

PRACTICAL information

PRACTICAL INFORMATION

Directory

GETTING THERE
By air
Milan's Malpensa airport is northern Italy's major air hub, making it easily accessible from anywhere in Europe – or the world. Flights from within Europe often use the smaller Linate airport.

Many people are aware that air travel emits CO_2 which contributes to climate change. You may be interested in the possibility of lessening the environmental impact of your flight through the charity Climate Care, which offsets your CO_2 by funding environmental projects around the world. Visit www.climatecare.org

▲ *Milan's Centrale railway station*

From the UK and Europe Ryanair (w www.ryanair.com) flies from Glasgow, Liverpool, Luton, Newcastle and Stansted to Bergamo's Orio al Serio airport, often at ridiculously low fares. Bergamo is a one-hour train ride (w www.trenitalia.it) from Milan's Porta Garibaldi station. EasyJet (w www.easyjet.com) serves both of Milan's airports from Gatwick and British Airways (w www.britishairways.com) has daily flights to Milan from Heathrow, Birmingham and Manchester. Alitalia (w www.alitalia.com) flies the same route with competitive fares.

From North America There are direct flights from the USA and Canada, from major US gateways to Milan's Malpensa airport via Alitalia (w www.alitalia.com), Continental (w www.continental.com) and several other airlines.

From Australia and New Zealand No direct flights are offered to any Italian city, so the best plan is to book the best price to a major European hub, with an onward connection to Milan.

Although there are fewer ready-made packages to Milan than to resort holiday havens, you can sometimes combine air fare, lodging and car hire into a money-saving package. Ask about the possibilities when booking flights. Especially when booking an entire package, it is wise to secure your trip with travel insurance. Most tour operators offer insurance options, or you can insure the trip independently to protect your investment.

By train

With the arrival of the Eurostar, Milan's Centrale station is on a direct rail link with Geneva, making the trip from London's Waterloo Station to Milan about 12 hours. Less pricey are conventional trains.

PRACTICAL INFORMATION

Milan is on the main line from Paris. Travel time is about five hours from Paris by Eurostar, seven by slower train. Italian trains run on time (w www.trenitalia.it). Be sure to have your ticket date-stamped in a machine on the platform of the station before boarding.

Travellers from outside Europe who plan to use trains should investigate the various multi-day train passes on Trenitalia and multi-country travel offered by Rail Europe (w www.raileurope.com). For travellers anywhere, Rail Europe offers a one-stop source of information, reservations and tickets, including Eurostar. Also of use is the **Thomas Cook European Rail Timetable** ❶ (UK) 01733 416477; (USA) 1 800 322 3834 w www.thomascookpublishing.com

By bus
Barring a lucky hit at a cut-rate air fare, the cheapest way to Milan from the UK is by bus, about 24 hours from London's Victoria Coach Station via Eurolines UK (❶ 08705 143219 w www.gobycoach.com or w www.eurolines.com).

By car
The Mont Blanc Tunnel speeds the trip across the Alps to Milan via the Piedmont region, along the A5 and A4 autostrade. Italy, like the rest of the continent, drives on the right-hand side of the road.

ENTRY FORMALITIES
Citizens of Ireland, USA, Canada, New Zealand, Australia, Singapore and Israel need only a valid passport to enter Italy and do not require visas for stays of up to 90 days. UK citizens may stay without a visa for an unlimited period. Citizens of South Africa must have visas to enter Italy.

DIRECTORY

EU citizens can bring goods for personal use when arriving from another EU country, but must observe the limits on tobacco (800 cigarettes) and spirits (10 litres over 22 per cent alcohol, 90 litres of wine). Limits for non-EU nationals are 200 cigarettes and one litre of spirits, two of wine.

MONEY

The euro (€) is the official currency in Italy. Currency exchange facilities and cashpoints are available at Bergamo, Linate and Malpensa airports.

Avoid carrying large amounts of cash, and if you must, hide it well in several concealed pockets and security pouches. Safer are traveller's cheques, accepted at banks, large hotels and by larger stores, but difficult to cash elsewhere. If possible, bring at least one major credit card; Visa is the most commonly accepted. Most small hotels, *agriturismo* properties and small restaurants do not accept cards. Expect trouble trying to cash Eurocheques, except in large banks.

Best for obtaining euros are credit or debit cards. Automated machines (*bancomat*) offer the best exchange rates, are found even in small towns and never close. Ask your card issuer before leaving home what network you can use in Italy and make sure that your PIN number can be used abroad. Banks are usually open 08.30–13.00 or 13.30, Mon–Fri. Try to have enough euros to last over weekends, when banks close and cashpoints may be out of money or out of order. Try to arrive with euros, especially on a weekend.

HEALTH, SAFETY & CRIME

In any large city you need to be aware of your surroundings, and avoid walking alone at night and in seedy neighbourhoods. Guard against pickpockets by carrying (well hidden) only the cash you need. Waist packs and bum bags label you as a tourist and make you a particular target anywhere. Be especially wary of crowded areas, such as train stations, buses and street markets, and avoid groups of small children who try to engage you in conversation. They are fast and work expertly in teams. Keep cameras firmly in your hand and the strap around your neck. As anywhere, don't leave cameras or handbags slung over the back of your chair in a restaurant.

Report any thefts immediately, and be sure to get a copy of the report (*denuncia*) for insurance. Police are of two varieties, the *carabinieri*, or national police, and the *vigili*, or local officers. Both are armed and can make arrests, but the *vigili* are usually more concerned with traffic and parking. They normally wear white uniforms in the summer, black in the winter. You can report a crime to either, but the paperwork must be completed at a *questura* (police station).

Drinking water is safe in Milan, as is food; it is wise to carry your favourite medication for an upset stomach, since travellers anywhere are more likely to eat and drink things their systems are unaccustomed to. Should you become ill or have an accident, medical care is quite good and free to EU residents who obtain a European Health Insurance Card (EHIC) from a local post office before leaving home. Non-EU residents should carry travellers' health insurance if their own coverage does not cover reimbursement, and should also consider emergency medical evacuation insurance. Emergency treatment at hospitals is free to everyone. For police and medical emergency numbers, see Emergencies, page 154.

As a pedestrian, always look both ways when crossing even on one-way streets, since bus lanes sometimes travel in the opposite direction. Those from left-hand drive countries need to be especially careful because traffic will be approaching from an unfamiliar direction. Motorised two-wheeled vehicles are common, and you should always be aware of these approaching between vehicles or emerging suddenly from alleyways.

OPENING HOURS

Major attractions open 08.30 or 09.00 to 19.00 or 19.30 with Monday closing. Smaller ones may have shorter hours, frequently closing for lunch. Hours are subject to change, so ask at the tourist office for the most up-to-date times (websites are notoriously out of date). Banks open 08.30–13.00 or 13.30, Mon–Fri. Shops generally open 09.00 or 10.00 until 19.00 or 19.30 Mon–Sat, smaller ones with an hour or two closing at lunch and Monday morning closing. Sunday openings are becoming more common. Street markets open about 07.00 and close around midday. Pharmacies are usually open 08.00–13.00 and 16.00–20.00, Mon–Sat, and a sign on the door will direct you to the nearest one open Sundays and nights.

TOILETS

Public buildings, such as museums, usually have clean toilets in the publicly accessible areas near the entrance (or will let you in to use one if you look desperate), and you will find occasional public facilities. But the fastest and easiest solution is to step into a bar or café and go directly to the back, following the sign 'toilet' or the universal symbols. These may not be entirely savoury affairs (always carry your own paper), but they are available. At public toilets, be prepared to pay a small fee, usually €0.50.

PRACTICAL INFORMATION

CHILDREN

Italians love children – and spoil them – but in Milan they rarely take them out to dinner in the evening, especially to upscale restaurants. These will not have appropriate chairs or children's portions and the staff may relegate you to a corner near the kitchen. Better to choose a small neighbourhood trattoria, where your whole family will be welcomed. Hotels can usually provide cots with advance notice, and you will rarely be charged for a child staying in a room with adults. Special infant needs, such as baby food and nappies, are available in supermarkets, but for a shorter stay it is easier to bring familiar brands from home.

Although not every place is suitable for all ages, the most kid-friendly sights in Milan are the Duomo roof, the armour collections at Castello Sforzesco and the natural history museum in Giardini Pubblici. Older children will enjoy the many working models in the **Museo Scienza e della Tecnica** and the interactive exhibits there that allow them to perform science experiments. When all else fails, head for one of Milan's many *gelato* counters.

Instead of trying to fit kids into Milan, it's better to make quick work of the city and head for safer ground. Castles are always a good bet, and there's a fine one as close as **Angera**. Maggiore also has swinging cable cars to the mountain top of **Mottorone** at Stresa, and at Como a creaking funicular climbs to **Brunate**. Older kids will get a kick out of the quirky free **transportation museum** at Ranco, where they can walk under the tracks to see how a funicular works and climb aboard trams and other vehicles. Boat rides on any of the lakes are a diversion,

> *Public transport comes in all shapes and sizes*

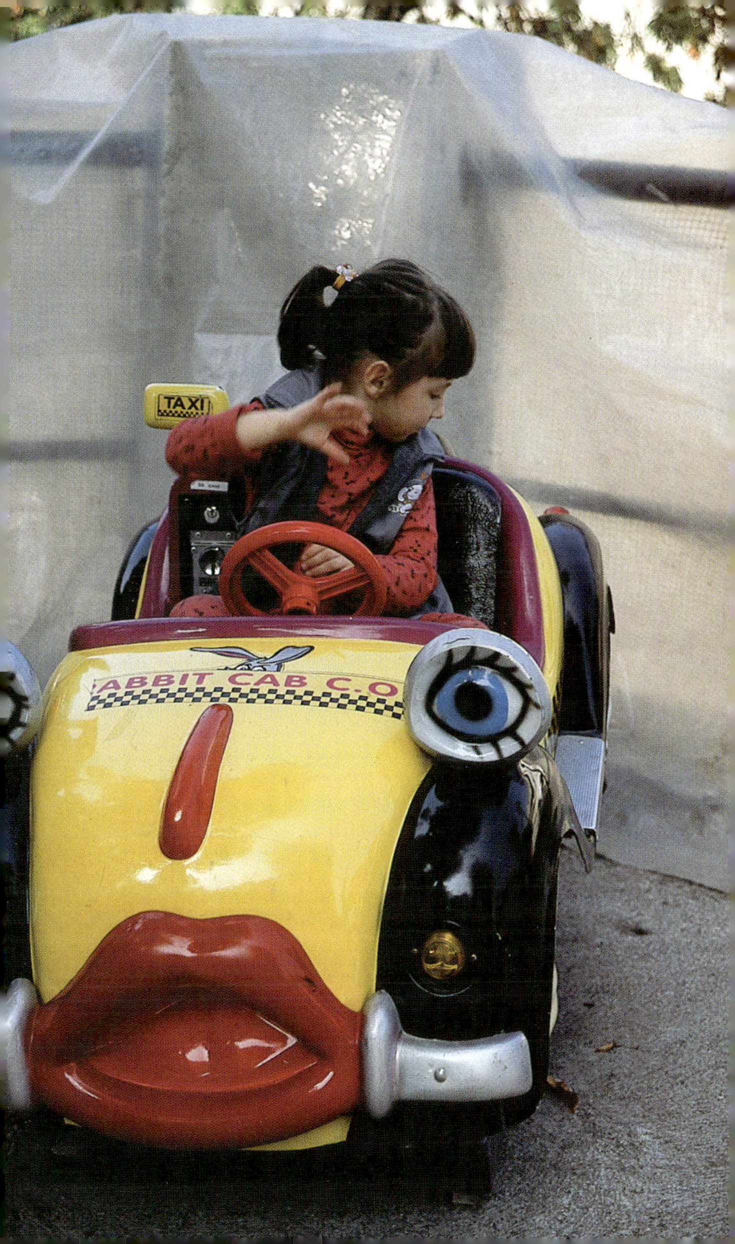
TAXI
ABBIT CAB C.O

PRACTICAL INFORMATION

especially on the boats that shuttle to islands: **Isola Comacina** in Lake Como and the **Borromean Islands** in Maggiore.

Natural wonders are especially exciting for kids, especially when they involve rivers doing really cool things, such as the one that carved the deep chasm of **Orrido di Bellano**. In the lake towns, look for kiddie playgrounds, with slides and climbing jungles, swings and other toys. These also provide a place to find playmates (who don't care if they don't speak the same language). Sometimes outdoor cafés will have a couple of plastic cars or other toys to occupy smallfry while parents sip an espresso.

Festivals always have children's activities and are colourful, lively occasions with music. Having a child with you is your best ticket to becoming part of the festivities instead of a spectator.

COMMUNICATIONS
Phones

All Milan numbers begin with 02, which must be dialed from inside or outside the city. Numbers vary between eight and nine digits, with a few shorter ones remaining. Numbers beginning with 800 are free phone. To use public telephones, buy a card (*carta telefonica*) from a *tabaccheria*, designated by a white T on a dark background. Hotel telephones usually carry a high surcharge, but not always, so ask at the desk.

To make an international call, dial 00, then the country code (UK = 44, Ireland = 353, US and Canada = 1, Australia = 61, New Zealand = 64, South Africa = 27) and number, omitting the initial zero in UK numbers. To call Milan from outside Italy, dial the international access code (00 in the UK and Ireland, 011 in the US), then Italy's country code of 39, then the number beginning with 02.

DIRECTORY

Mobile phone numbers begin with 3; if you see an old number with the prefix 03, omit the zero. Your UK, New Zealand and Australian mobile phone will work in Italy; US and Canadian cell phones will not. Travellers from those countries can solve this easily with a universal mobile from Mobal, a UK firm with cutting-edge expertise in international communications. These mobiles work anywhere in the world, with a permanent UK number that travels with you (UK ☎ 01543 426 999 ☎ 01543 426 126 ⓦ www.mobell.co.uk; US ☎ 888 888 9162 (free call) or 212 785 5800 ⓦ www.mobalrental.com)

Post

Italian postal service is quite reliable. For letters and postcards you can buy stamps (*francobolli*) at a *tabaccheria*, and for special services you can go to a post office (**Poste e Telecommunicazioni (Central Post Office)** ⊙ Via Cordusio 4, west of Piazza del Duomo ☎ 02 8056 812). If you pay extra for *prioritaria*, your card or letter should arrive the next day in Italy, within three days in the UK and about five days elsewhere. Rates change often, so ask at the *tabaccheria* selling the stamps.

Internet

Internet is increasingly available, both in hotels and internet points and cafés around the city. Most upper-end hotels have in-room points, others will likely allow you to plug into their phone systems. Tourist information offices and kiosks can provide lists of internet cafés and public access points such as libraries.

PRACTICAL INFORMATION

ELECTRICITY

Electrical appliances used in the UK will work in Italy, but those from the US and Canada will need an adaptor to convert from 110v to 220v. However, travellers from the UK and outside Europe will need to have plug adapters for sockets using two round pins.

TRAVELLERS WITH DISABILITIES

Milan is the happy exception to the enormous challenges much of Italy presents to those with limited mobility. Several of the city museums are handicapped accessible, including Civico Museo di Arte Contemporanio, Galleria d'Arte Enrico, Museo Teatrale alla Scala and Palazzo Reale. Milan also has one of the best sites for information on access and assistance for handicapped travellers, ⓦ www.milanopertutti.it. The main site has an English option but some of the links are only in Italian.

Airport assistance: the Sala Amica provides assistance on check-in, boarding and disembarkation at both of Milan's major airports. This includes not only the loading process but waiting arrangements as well. Wheelchairs are carried free. Check-in is at the Sala Amica. Make arrangements to be met when booking your flight.
ⓐ Malpensa Terminal 1 ⓣ 02 5858 0298 ⓐ Malpensa Terminal 2
ⓣ 02 5858 3266, ⓐ Linate ⓣ 02 716 659

City transportation: Buses 39, 48, 49, 50, 54, 56, 57, 58, 65, 73, 78, 83, 84, 94 are fully handicapped accessible with low entry levels. This is an ongoing programme and buses on other lines are being replaced with low-access vehicles.

DIRECTORY

Access to trains: Look for the booklet *I Servizi per la Clientel a Disabile* at any railway station. It lists the stations with disabled reception centres (*Centro di Accoglienza Disabili*). For assistance at **Stazione Centrale** call ❶ 02 6707 0958. The ticket office and the waiting areas are accessible and the platforms are accessed by lift. It is a busy station, so allow extra time. **Stazione Garibaldi** (north- and west-bound trains) has a reception station for disabled travellers (@ Centro di Accoglienza Disabili ❶ 02 6371 6105 or 02 6371 6274). **Ferovie Nord** (Como and Varese) station at Via Cardona has accessible ticket offices and platform. Some new high speed trains are accessesed at platform level. Information and assistance can be arranged by calling ❶ 02 202 22 ⓦ www.ferrovienord.it

Elevator equipped vans: Make reservations at least 48 hours in advance to schedule the services of these taxi-vans equipped with wheelchair elevators. Alatha ❶ 02 5796 41 ❶ 02 5796 4210, Missione Handicap ❶ 02 4229 0549 ❶ 02 4895 8413, C.T.A. ❶ 02 3559 360, 02 3574 768 ❶ 02 3320 0456, Stella Cometa ❶ 02 8942 3078, 02 8320 0752 ❶ 02 5810 1064. For Monza, Monza Viaggi 2000 ❶ 03 9202 4836 ❶ 03 9202 4852 ⓦ www.monza2000.com

TOURIST INFORMATION
Tourist offices – Milan
Azienda di Promozione Turistica (APT) The main office is in the Piazza Duomo at Via Marconi 1. Be sure to look at its 1930s art deco architecture. ⓛ 08.45–13.00, 14.00–17.45 Mon–Fri, 09.00–13.00, 14.00–16.45 Sat & Sun ❶ 02 7252 4300 ❶ 02 7252 4350

PRACTICAL INFORMATION

Information points – Milan
Stazione Centrale (Central Rail Station) Look for it near the Gran Bar on the first floor, and be sure to look at the 1931 architecture inside and out. ⏰ 08.00–19.00 Mon–Fri, 09.00–12.30, 13.30–1800 Sat & Sun ☎ 02 7252 4360

Castello Sforzesco This office is a joint operation of the local Chamber of Commerce and the Province of Milano so it is a good place to get local and regional material. 📍 Piazza Castello 1 ⏰ 09.00–18.00 Mon–Sat ☎ 02 8058 0615

Tourist offices – the lakes
Como APT 📍 Piazza Cavour 17, Como ☎ 031 274 064 or 031 269 712 🌐 www.lakecomo.com ⏰ 09.00–13.00, 14.00–18.00 Mon–Sat ℹ A smaller kiosk is located on the south side of the Duomo

Bellagio IAT 📍 Lungolago Mazzini, Bellagio ☎ 031 950 204 🌐 www.bellagiolakecomo.com ⏰ 09.00–12.00 Apr–Oct, 15.00–18.00 Nov–Mar, closed Tues & Sun

Tremezzo Information 📍 Via Regina 3, Tremezzo ☎ 0344 404 93 🌐 www.tremezzina.com ⏰ 09.00–12.00, 15.30–18.30 Mon–Wed, Fri–Sat, May–Sept

Distretto Turistico 📍 Via Principe Tomaso 70, Stresa ☎ 03 2330 416 🌐 www.distrettolaghi.it

Ente Turistico Lago Maggiore (for the Swiss sector) ☎ 091 791 0091 🌐 www.maggiore.ch ℹ When calling Switzerland, use country code 41

DIRECTORY

Lake transport
Navigazione Lago Maggiore (information on water transport on Lake Maggiore) ⓐ Viale le Baracca 1, Arona ⓣ 03 2223 3200
ⓦ www.navigazionelaghi.it

Useful websites
ⓦ www.italiantourism.com The Italian national tourism (Ente Nazionale Italiano per il Turismo, or ENIT) site, with general information on travel in Italy, as well as regional coverage.
ⓦ www.milanoinfotourist.com Milan's tourism website
ⓦ www.ciaomilano.it By far the most useful site on Milan, with descriptions of museums and sites, restaurant and entertainment listings and helpful suggestions.

Italian overseas tourist offices
Italian Tourist Office ⓐ 1 Princes Street, London W1R 8AY, England ⓣ 020 7408 1254 ⓦ www.italiantouristboard.co.uk
Italian Government Tourist Board ⓐ 630 Fifth Avenue, Suite 1565, New York, NY 10111, USA ⓣ 212 245 5618
Italian Government Tourist Board ⓐ 175 Bloor Street East, Suite 907 – South Tower, Toronto, ON M4W 3R8, Canada ⓣ 416 925 4882, Brochures 416 925 3870
Italian Government Tourist Office ⓐ 44 Market Street, Level 6, Sydney, NSW 2000, Australia ⓣ 02 9262 1666
ⓦ www.italiantourism.com.au
Italian Tourist Office ⓐ Italian Embassy, 796 George Avenue, Arcadia 0083, Pretoria, South Africa ⓣ 012 430 55 41
Italian Tourist Office ⓐ Italian Embassy, 34–38 Grant Road, Thorndon, Wellington, NZ ⓣ 04 4947 173

PRACTICAL INFORMATION

Useful phrases

Although English is spoken in many tourist locations in Milan, these words and phrases may come in handy. See also the phrases for specific situations in other parts of this book.

English	Italian	Approx. pronunciation
BASICS		
Yes	Sì	*See*
No	No	*Noh*
Please	Per favore	*Perr fahvawreh*
Thank you	Grazie	*Grahtsyeh*
Hello	Salve	*Sahlveh*
Goodbye	Arrivederci	*Arreevehderrchee*
Excuse me	Scusi	*Skoozee*
Sorry	Scusi	*Skoozee*
That's okay	Va bene	*Vah behneh*
To	A	*Ah*
From	Da	*Dah*
I don't speak Italian	Non parlo italiano	*Nawn parrlaw itahlyahnaw*
Do you speak English?	Parla inglese?	*Parrla eenglehzeh?*
Good morning	Buon giorno	*Booawn geeyawrnaw*
Good afternoon	Buon pomeriggio	*Booawn pawmehreehdjaw*
Good evening	Buonasera	*Booawnah sehrah*
Goodnight	Buonanotte	*Booawnah nawtteh*
My name is ...	Mi chiamo ...	*Mee kyahmaw ...*
DAYS & TIMES		
Monday	Lunedì	*Loonehdee*
Tuesday	Martedì	*Marrtehdee*
Wednesday	Mercoledì	*Merrcawlehdee*
Thursday	Giovedì	*Jawvehdee*
Friday	Venerdì	*Venerrdee*
Saturday	Sabato	*Sahbahtaw*
Sunday	Domenica	*Dawmehneeca*
Morning	Mattino	*Mahtteenaw*
Afternoon	Pomeriggio	*Pawmehreedjaw*
Evening	Sera	*Sehra*
Night	Notte	*Notteh*
Yesterday	Ieri	*Yeree*

USEFUL PHRASES

English	Italian	Approx. pronunciation
Today	Oggi	*Odjee*
Tomorrow	Domani	*Dawmahnee*
What time is it?	Che ore sono?	*Keh awreh sawnaw?*
It is …	Sono le …	*Sawnaw leh …*
09.00	Nove	*Noveh*
Midday	Mezzogiorno	*Metsawjorrnaw*
Midnight	Mezzanotte	*Metsanotteh*

NUMBERS

English	Italian	Approx. pronunciation
One	Uno	*Oonaw*
Two	Due	*Dweh*
Three	Tre	*Treh*
Four	Quattro	*Kwahttraw*
Five	Cinque	*Cheenkweh*
Six	Sei	*Say*
Seven	Sette	*Setteh*
Eight	Otto	*Ottaw*
Nine	Nove	*Noveh*
Ten	Dieci	*Dyehchee*
Eleven	Undici	*Oondeechee*
Twelve	Dodici	*Dawdeechee*
Twenty	Venti	*Ventee*
Fifty	Cinquanta	*Cheenkwahnta*
One hundred	Cento	*Chentaw*

MONEY

English	Italian	Approx. pronunciation
I would like to change these traveller's cheques/this currency	Vorrei cambiare questi assegni turistici/ questa valuta	*Vawrray cahmbyahreh kwestee assenee tooreesteechee/kwesta vahloota*
Where is the nearest ATM?	Dov'è il bancomat più vicino?	*Dawveh eel bankomaht pyoo veecheenaw?*
Do you accept credit cards?	Accettate carte di credito?	*Achetahteh kahrrteh dee krehdeehtaw?*

SIGNS & NOTICES

English	Italian	Approx. pronunciation
Airport	Aeroporto	*Ahaerrhawpawrrtaw*
Railway station	Stazione ferroviaria	*Stahtsyawneh ferrawvyarya*
Platform	Binario	*Binahriaw*
Smoking/non-smoking	Per fumatori/non fumatori	*Perr foomahtawree/non foomahtawree*
Toilets	Gabinetti	*Gabinettee*
Ladies/Gentlemen	Signore/Signori	*Seenyawreh/Seenyawree*
Subway	Metropolitana	*Metrawpawleetahna*

PRACTICAL INFORMATION

Emergencies

No traveller wants to need any of these emergency numbers, but it's comforting to know that they are handy in case you should need one.

POLICE
Should you need to report a theft (*furto*), missing person or any other matter for the police, go to the *questura*, or police station. If insurance is involved, ask for a *denuncia*, a stamped form that you must have for filing claims.

Questura (Main Police Station) ❸ Via Fatebenefratelli 11, west of the Giardini Pubblici ❶ 02 622 61, English speaking 02 863 701

Stazione Centrale (Central Station) There is a handy sub-station in the main railway station, useful for reporting thefts.

Stresa Police: Carabinieri ❸ Via Carducci ❶ 0323 301 18; local police: 0323 932 994

To reach the police in an emergency, dial **112**.

MEDICAL
Should you become ill while travelling, you have several sources of information on English-speaking doctors. If you can reach your consulate, they can provide a list, or you can go prepared with the appropriate pages from the directory published by IAMAT. The International Association of Medical Assistance for travellers is a non-profit organisation that provides medical information on health-related travel issues all over the world, as well as a list of

❶ *A street musician*

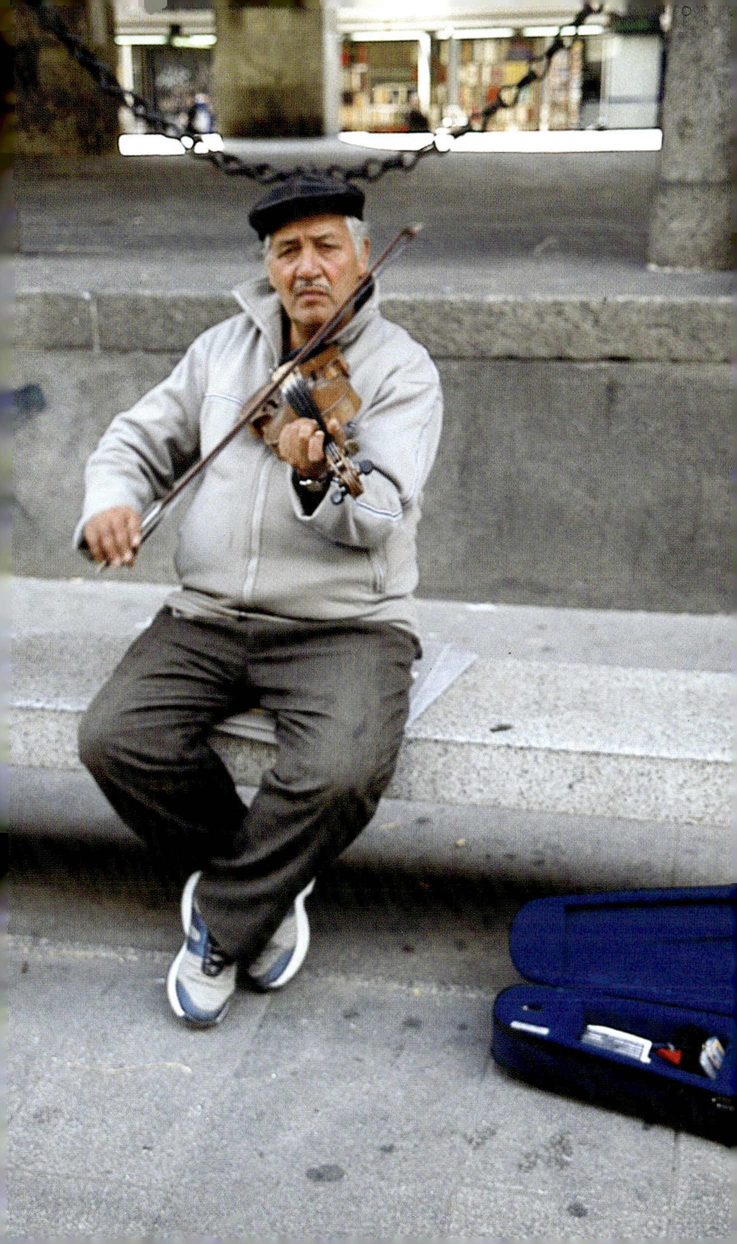

PRACTICAL INFORMATION

English speaking doctors (W www.iamat.org). Hospital accident and emergency departments (ask for the *pronto soccorso*) are open 24 hours daily, and must treat you free of charge in an emergency.

Ospedale Maggiore Polyclinico a short distance from the Duomo, a Via Francesco Sforza 35, use the Duomo or Mission Metro stops. 02 556 812, 800 638 638 W www.policlinico.mi.it

Medical Emergency Dial **118**, a free call to ambulances and emergency medical care.

AUTOMOBILE
Members of the Automobile Association in the UK have reciprocal privileges with the Italian Automobile Association. For roadside assistance and breakdowns, contact ACI Breakdown Service 116

LOST & FOUND
Aeroporto della Malpensa 02 7485 4215
Aeroporto Linate 02 7010 2094

EMERGENCY PHRASES

Help! Aiuto! *Ahyootaw!* **Fire!** Al fuoco! *Ahl fooawcaw!*
Stop! Ferma! *Fairmah!*

Call an ambulance/a doctor/the police/the fire service!
Chiamate un'ambulanza/un medico/la polizia/i pompieri!
Kyahmahteh oon ahmboolahntsa/oon mehdeecaw/la pawleetsya/ee pompee-ehree!

EMERGENCIES

Aeroporto Internazionale di Orio al Serio ☎ 035 326 323
Stazione Centrale At the stored luggage station ☎ 02 6371 2667
City Lost and Found @ Via Fruili 30, south of the Duomo
☎ 02 551 6141

CONSULATES & EMBASSIES

In general, it is a consulate that handles emergencies of travelling citizens, not the embassy. But if there is no consulate in a country, embassies take over these responsibilities. Your consulate or embassy should be the first place you turn to if a passport is lost, after reporting it to the police. Consulates can also provide lists of English-speaking doctors and dentists and find you an English-speaking lawyer.

British Consulate General @ Via S. Paolo 7, 20121 Milano
☎ 02 723 001, after office hours 335 810 6857 ℻ 02 864 65081
ⓦ www.britishembassy.gov.uk/italy
American Consulate General @ Via Principe Amedeo 2, 20121 Milano
☎ 02 626 88520 ℻ 02 659 6561 ⓦ www.usembassy.it
Australian Consulate General @ 3rd Floor, Via Borgogna 2, 20122
Milano ☎ 02 777 041 ℻ 02 777 04242 ⓦ www.australian-embassy.it
New Zealand Embassy @ Via Zara 28, 00198 Roma ☎ 06 441 7171
℻ 06 440 2984
South African Consul General @ Vicolo S. Giovanni sul Muro 4, 20121
Milano ☎ 02 885 8581 ⓦ www.sudafrica.it
Embassy of Canada, Consular Section @ Via Zara 30, 00198 Roma
☎ 06 445 981, automated information line 06 445 983 937
℻ 06 445 983 750

INDEX

A
accommodation 34–39, 117–119, 134–136
air travel 49, 138–139
airports 48, 138, 148
Angera 120, 122
Arona 122
arts *see* culture
Ascona 128–129
ATMs 141

B
banks 141
bars, clubs & discos 28–29, 45, 70, 72–73, 86–87, 97–98, 100, 115, 117
Bellagio 105
Bramante, Donato 92–93
Brera 74
Brissago 129
Brunate 105–106
bus travel 48–49, 53, 56, 140

C
cafés 84–85, 98, 114
Calde 126
canals 88
car hire 56
Casa degli Omenoni 58
Casa del Manzoni 58
Castello Sforzesco 44, 74
Cernobbio 106
children 143–146
Cimitero Monumentale 45, 76
Civiche Raccolte d'Arte Antica del Castello 81
Civiche Raccolte di Arte Applicata 81
Civico Museo Archeologico 45, 80–81
coffee 24
Como 106, 108
consulates 156–157
credit & debit cards 141
crime 34–35, 52, 141–142
culture 18–20, 64–65, 72, 80–82, 94–95, 111
customs & duty 140–141

D
disabilities, travellers with 148–149
driving 49, 52, 140, 156
Duomo 46, 60–61

E
electricity 147
embassies 156
emergencies 142, 154, 156–157
entertainment 28–29
see also nightlife
events 8–11, 133

F
fashion 12–13, 22, 63–64, 66, 68, 82, 83–84, 95
ferry travel 102
festivals 8, 9, 10
fitness 30–31
food & drink 24, 25–26
football 32–33, 94

G
Galleria Vittorio Emanuele II 46, 61
Giardini Alpina 127
Giardini Pubblici 62
golf 31–32

H
health 142, 154, 156
history 14–15
horse riding 32
hotels 34–39, 117–119, 134–136

I
insurance 138–139
internet 147

Isola Bella 124–125
Isola Brissago 129
Isola Comacina 108
Isola Madre 125
Isola Pescatore 125–126
Isole Borromeo 122

L
La Rinascente 47, 66–67
Lake Como 102–104, 109
Lake Maggiore 120
language 23, 27, 53, 152–153, 157
The Last Supper (Leonardo da Vinci) 79
Laveno 126
Leonardo da Vinci 79, 88, 94
L'Eremo di Santa Caterina del Sasso Ballaro 126
lifestyle 16–17
Locarno 129

M
markets 22, 113, 131
Metro 53
Michelangelo 44, 81
money 141
Museo Civico 111
Museo dei Transporti 120, 122
Museo Didattico della Seta 111
Museo La Scala 64
Museo Nazionale della Scienza e della Tecnologia Leonardo da Vinci 94
Museo Poldi Pezzoli 64–65
Museo Zucchi 65
music 18–20, 29, 72–73, 86–87, 100, 117, 133

158

INDEX

N
Navigli 88
nightlife 28–29, 70–73, 85–87, 98–100, 115–117, 131–133

O
opening hours 22, 143
opera 18, 72
Orrido di Bellano 110
Orto Botanico di Brera 77

P
Palazzo Bagatti Valsecchi 65
Palazzo Borromeo 125
Palazzo dell'Arte (Triennale) 77
Palazzo Reale 62–63
Parco Sempione 77
passports & visas 140
phones 146–147
Piazza del Duomo 46, 52
Piazza Mercanti 90
Pinacoteca Ambrosiana 95
Pinacoteca di Brera 82
police 142, 154
post 147
public holidays 11
public transport 48–49, 53–56, 102, 139–140, 148–149

Q
Quadrilatero della Moda 22, 63–64, 68

R
rail stations 139
rail travel 48–49, 102, 139–140, 148–149
Reserva Naturale di Fondo Toce 128
restaurants 25, 26–27, 70–71, 85–86, 99, 115–116, 131–133
Rondanini Pietà (Michelangelo) 44, 81

S
safety 34–35, 52, 141–143
San Ambrogio 92
San Bernadino alle Ossa 64
San Carlo Borromeo (statue) 122
San Lorenzo Maggiore 90
San Sebastiano 90–91
Santa Maria delle Grazie 79
Santa Maria presso San Satiro 92–93
Sant'Eustorgio 92
seasons 8
shopping 22–23, 46, 47, 61, 66–68, 82–84, 95, 97, 111, 113, 129–130
silk 111, 113
sport 31–33, 94
Stadio Giuseppe Meazza (San Siro) 94
Stazione Centrale 34–35
Stresa 127
Swiss Maggiore 128

T
taxi-vans 149
taxis 48–49, 56
Teatro alla Scala 18, 62, 72
time differences 48
tipping 27
toilets 143
Torre Branco 78
Tort de' spus 79–80
tourist information 149–151
trams 53, 56
Tremezzina Riviera 108–110

V
Varenna 110
Verbania 127–128
Villa Balbianello 109–110
Villa Carlotta 109
Villa d'Este 106
Villa Pallavicino 127
Villa Reale 45, 65
Villa Táranto 128

W
weather 8
wine 26

ACKNOWLEDGEMENTS & FEEDBACK

The publishers would like to thank Stillman Rogers for supplying all the copyright photographs for this book except for page 33 which was kindly supplied by Archivo Fotografico I.A.T. Ufficio Informazioni e Accoglienza Turistica della Provincia di Milano.

Copy editor: Natasha Reed
Proofreader: Lynn Bresler

Send your thoughts to
books@thomascook.com

- Found a great bar, club, shop or must-see sight that we don't feature?
- Like to tip us off about any information that needs updating?
- Want to tell us what you love about this handy little guidebook and more importantly how we can make it even handier?

Then here's your chance to tell all! Send us ideas, discoveries and recommendations today and then look out for your valuable input in the next edition of this title. As an extra 'thank you' from Thomas Cook Publishing, you'll be automatically entered into our exciting monthly prize draw.

Send an email to the above address (stating the book's title) or write to: CitySpots Project Editor, Thomas Cook Publishing, PO Box 227, The Thomas Cook Business Park, Unit 18, Coningsby Road, Peterborough PE3 8SB, UK.